Carlos Camargo

HAPPY AND UNBOUND

MAKE TIME YOUR BEST ALLY

Skinny Brown Dog Media

Published by Skinny Brown Dog Media
Atlanta, Punta del Este
www.skinnybrowndogmedia.com
Distributed by Skinny Brown Dog Media
Translation Services: Skinny Brown Dog Media
Developmental Editing and Design by Eric G. Reid
Content Editing by Timothy Swiney

Spanish Edition Published by PanHouse Casa Editorial
www.editorialpanhouse.com
CEO: Jonathan Somoza
Production Manager: Paola Morales

Publisher's Cataloging-in-Publication Data

Paperback: ISBN 978-1957506-12-8
EBook: ISBN 978-1957506-13-5
Spanish Edition ISBN 979-8418244116

This book is an authorized translation of *Feliz y sin ataduras: Haz del tiempo tu mejor aliado* written by Carlos Camargo, originally published in Spanish in February 2022 by Editorial PanHouse.

The translation team at Skinny Brown Dog Media has worked closely with the author to preserve his voice while making his story and wisdom available to the English audience.

Enjoy!

DEDICATION

I want to dedicate these pages, which were made by hand, feeling, memories and a lot of love, to many people who have contributed to my daily life, because with them I have learned the value of life. I would like to name them all, many already know who they are. People who showed me their encouragement and drive and got involved in this dream that today has become a reality.

I want these lines to be a magical act of love. First to God and my family, but also to Rosana Ordóñez, who gave me the first opportunity.

To Gloria Fuentes, for spoiling me in my ideas and escapades.

To mommy Devorah, for having given me a beautiful and very talented woman. my Chiqui Delgado. To you, my heart and soul for so many years of beautiful friendship.

To so many friends in the media, who always reached out to me and opened their hearts to me.

To Larry Brown II, thank you for your knowledge for my growth and success.

Especially to my publishing house, Bloque Dearmas, for always being my accomplice and allowing me to grow among newspapers and magazines.

To Martin Dearmas Jr. for believing in me.

And I end by dedicating each page to tomorrow, because it will always be better than today and yesterday.

ACKNOWLEDGMENTS

To God and my family.

Gratitude to the Creator, to God, because he guides my steps. And to my family, because each one of them are my support, my inspiration, my identity and my principles. My mother, unique and consistent. My father, example at all times. My brother, unconditional support. To my nephews: Luis, Carlos Enrique and Luis Carlos, for giving me reasons to continue. To all of you from the fibers of my heart: thank you!

Being thankful is something my parents have always instilled in me since I was a child. I love to be thankful. To God, because even though I don't have much, I have everything. Sometimes I turn to the sky or look at the plains, observe a beautiful and chromatic sunset or simply close my eyes and say: I know it was you, my Lord, who took care of giving me so much happiness and my way of living.

I thank life for so many good things, my friends, my artists, for believing in me; my colleagues, for so much support; my new friends in the United States who opened their hearts to me and made me part of their family.

To Larry Brown II for giving me so much support and for being that staff of life, an angel of the color of the night. Grateful for your teaching for my personal and professional growth.

Thank you for teaching me that the most important thing is to live with faith, hope and full of joy and happiness.

Infinite thanks to the Almighty for allowing me to write these lines about my stay on this planet and to be able, in some way, to inspire others to be happy. Because life is like an animated book, with friends who are in a couple of pages, others in a chapter and others, in my case most of them, present in the whole story. Thank you all.

About the Author

Carlos Camargo was born in Caracas, Venezuela in 1967. He was trained as a journalist from an early age, when his perseverance and childhood dream of becoming an entertainment reporter led him to the desk of one of the most outstanding journalists in Venezuela, Rossana Ordóñez, who directed the current affairs and political magazines *Momento* and *Bohemia*, published by Bloque Dearmas, who believed in him and added him to her team of editors, even though he was only seventeen years old.

Soon after, Camargo joined the team of entertainment, showbiz and lifestyle magazines of the same publishing house, under the direction of Gloria Fuentes, consolidating himself as a proactive and dynamic journalist.

His perseverance and creativity positioned him as general producer of Bloque Dearmas magazines, a task that led him to become one of the most influential figures in the field of fashion and beauty, working alongside emblematic personalities such as Osmel Sousa, Roland Carreño and Mariela Centeno.

Simultaneously, he coordinated the photographic direction of editorial products for *El Nacional* and took his first steps as an artistic representative, having worked throughout his career with stars such as Celia Cruz, Shakira, J Balvin, Olga Tañón, Luis Enrique, Romeo Santos, Franco De Vita, Rummy Olivo, Luis Silva and Mariana Vega, among many others. Today he is the communications advisor to artists such as Oscar D'León, Chiquinquirá Delgado, Porfi Baloa, and Mandy Corrente.

Carlos Camargo, who has also worked as a public relations officer for organizations such as the Eurobuilding Hotel, has received awards such as Musa de Oro, Tacarigua de Oro, El Emperador, and has been recognized by organizations such as the Miranda State Government, with the Orden Buen Comunicador Social, in its First Class, Venezuelan Business Club, Oscar de la Renta, Fundación Cultural Tocando la Fama, and the Movimiento Ser Bueno es Bueno (Being Good is Good Movement) in Miami, among others.

Carlos Camargo currently lives in the United States, where he directs the *Notiamérica* portal and *Alta Esfera* magazine; he edits *Millenions* and *LatinGuia* magazines in Miami. He is a columnist for *El Venezolano* in its Madrid, Miami and Dominican Republic versions; he is a contributor to the portals *NotiExpress Color*, *Qué Vacilón*, and is a columnist for the agency *Authority*, which distributes content to more than fifty media outlets in the United States in English.

In addition, she continues to be a columnist for the *2001 Diario* del Bloque Dearmas and although it seems that she has no time to spare, she lives with happiness as a premise, traveling and enjoying the simplest details of life. How does she do it? He explains it in this, his first book, where he shares with a magnetic anecdotal capacity, how his experience has been making his dream come true so that others can also achieve it.

Adriana Terán H.

FOREWORD

My heroes are those who do not give up, those who enter through the window when they cannot find a door. Those beings that fear does not paralyze them and if it has to be done, it is done, even if it is with fear. Those people who dream big with the certainty that this desire will be fulfilled. Beings that nothing stops them, and that make difficulties their main engine. That is the author of this book. That's how I remember him, that's how he is and that's how he will always be.

Without a doubt, life belongs to those who take risks. Nothing resembles happiness more than savoring an achievement that has cost us sweat and tears. And if it is also shared and serves as an inspiration to others, the gift is immense and makes it all make sense.

If you are one of those who are full of excuses to work for what you dream of, this book is not for you. Its author has faced countless difficulties and with firmness and determination he has always moved forward, and that is precisely its message. No matter how big or distant your goal, your circumstances or your environment, discipline, rigor and hard work always pay off.

I met Carlos so long ago that my memory tricks me and I get the years mixed up, but what I am sure of is that it was love at first sight. I wanted to be his friend, his inexhaustible energy and his winning spirit simply hooked me.

If he has given me anything, it has been an unconditional friendship that is proof against years, countries and zip codes. He is always there, with his helping hand for me and for all those who need his support. His dedication is total and absolute, and he makes it clear in these pages. He exemplifies that phrase that says, "if we don't come for everything, we might as well not come at all".

I hope this journey of letters gives you inspiration and enthusiasm, as it does to all of us who are immersed in it.

Chiquinquirá Delgado

Actress, model and television presenter

COMMENTS

"I think Carlos Camargo is an example of overcoming, cf making his way to new horizons, of conquering and meeting new challenges. One of the things I value the most is that, although so many years have passed since I read about him, I see that he is still a grateful person, full of desire, and above all with a great smile that is contagious to everyone. I wish you all the success in the world, my dear Carlos, and may God bless your path even more. I love you very much and thank you for always being such a good vibe with me."

Marjorie De Sousa
Actress and Singer

"Whatever they tell me Carlos Camargo is going to do does not surprise me and I believe it. I know him so well that nothing surprises me about him. I saw this news about his book coming a long time ago. Everything he has proposed in his life for the last forty years, when I met him, has crystallized in a short time.

His professional life is full of anecdotes and episodes that well-known colleagues would have liked to experience. From the moment he arrived at Bloque Dearmas I knew he had a huge future, I knew he was going to become someone important in the media. And he did it in record time. My sister, Gloria Fuentes, followed in his footsteps and became his right hand in the selection of material for the many magazine covers he directed. Carlitos was born with a star in his hand. How valuable he is! And as a friend, he is great too."

Rafael Fuentes Jr.
Journalist

"Life belongs to the brave and to those who dare". One of the pillars I built thanks to my media guru. If you want to be different this book is for you."

Vivian Sleiman
Lecturer, Coach and Author of the best seller
Virgin at 30
The Power of Your Spirit

"Carlos Camargo is truly amazing! He still has the same spirit he had when I met him, when he was a young boy just starting to work as a writer and producer for Venezuela's top entertainment press institution: Bloque Dearmas". From the day I met him, he accompanied me in the most important events of my life, until my wedding with Eduardo Marturet in Venezuela.

Since then, he was my press officer and I still have this material from my beginnings, impeccably written with that poetic touch that characterizes him. He was a fundamental base to achieve my dreams. Apart from his unique gift, he is very noble and so humble that it is no wonder we call you prince. You are the prince of the media and I am infinitely grateful for you. I adore you forever!"

Athina klioumi de Marturet
Model and Actress

"To read his book will be to be enraptured by his many experiences, like reliving a movie that only someone like Carlos Camargo can have accumulated from his great experiences with famous show business figures. Camargo is a tireless being full of good energy. The only thing that surpasses his great professionalism is his gift for people, which has been his passport to success. He is the only journalist to whom important show business figures tell their lives without fear that he will reveal their secrets, he is an excellent friend, so I recommend that you read him, I will be the first, because his book has unique anecdotes and memories, since, in addition, Carlos has a photographic memory, which I am sure he captured in his book. Finally, let me tell you something, you know Camargo and you will never forget him? He is my star journalist."

Katty Tahan
Editor of *Alta Esfera* Magazine

"My way", the famous song popularized by the unforgettable Frank Sinatra, is the first thing that comes to mind when I think of my great and dear friend Carlos Camargo. And the fact is that he has made his life, his profession and his long career "his way". Without fears, doubts or insecurities... Always with his unique character, full of positivity, self-confidence and his jocular way of looking at life.

I affectionately call him Dorian Gray, and those of us who know him well know that he also has his Peter Pan touch. The big boy with the eternal smile, but the smart man who is not afraid to face new challenges. I am sure this will not be his only book. There will be other books to come because "Camarguito" is, without a doubt, unstoppable."

Minty Sanabria
Journalist

12

Table of Contents

PREFACE

Life is the result of the sum of little things done, undone or undone. Many live it with everything done, without sweat, without tears, without suffering. Others, on the other hand, undo their villas and castles to make of their lives their own hells; but there are those who make their lives from their dreams, their desires and their passions. I belong to that group, to that particular population.

I can describe myself as a hard-working, hard-working, educated man, and I could go on adding other adjectives that could add more data to my description. However, that is not the idea; what I want is for you to know more about me, not that one, the one in the description, which makes me more common than particular. Thank God that's so, because that means there are many good people in this world, but I didn't come here for you to know the life of an average "good person". Believe me, without wishing to sound boastful, I break the profile of the common man.

The purpose of this book is for you to meet Carlos Camargo, the most joyful and unique human being who is willing to tell you how he has managed to be happy, productive and successful, besides having a particular way of living, a model that can serve as a reference for other people who want to celebrate life, inside and outside the workplace, while still being effective and competent in what he does.

I am not a man who has inherited some fortune or who has accumulated wealth, I am simply a professional who works *online,* with many years in the same area, with the difference that I do not live for work, but I work to keep myself busy, to cover my lifestyle, to do what I want, and I am sure that many will want to know how I do it, because the work rhythm they carry in the company they work for absorbs them in such a way that they no longer have moments to share with family, friends or to enjoy the tranquility that solitude brings.

Through these lines I will reveal to you the steps I followed to live my life with full freedom, so you will take away the right of others to put a price on your knowledge or to want to pigeonhole you in schedules and clocks.

You are the owner of your time, of what you know and, like me, you have to set limits to those who hire you, guaranteeing the quality of your work, to gain confidence and recognition from others who want to gain from your work.

I can only tell you that you should always visualize what you want, because it is the hidden power that we human beings have to reach the unattainable. I did it since I was a child and today I live as I always dreamed, I work what I always wanted to work, I do what I always wanted to do and I am the happiest man on Earth. So you do it too, and if you don't know how, I will tell you throughout this book how I did it.

This time let me

be happy,

nothing has happened to anyone,

I am nowhere to be found,

happens only

that I am happy

on all sides

of the heart, walking,

sleeping or writing.

What am I going to do to him,

I am happy.

Excerpt from *Ode to Happiness*
Pablo Neruda

CHAPTER 1

A Non-traditional Young Man

PASSION FOR A DREAM

When you have a dream, a longing, you have to work tirelessly to make it come true, because dreaming and wishing alone is not enough. This is how I discovered my passion and my talent. As a child, when I learned to read and write, I wanted to write everything on every piece of paper I could get my hands on. If I had a pencil in my hand, I began to feel an uncontrollable desire to write. It was almost an obsession that took hold of me.

I distinctly remember that I began to show the glow of my grace at the age of eight. I began to unconsciously cultivate my love for the written word, writing the songs of my favorite artists, something that I have considered the magic chip that has brought me to this present day. Although I consider myself a self-confessed music lover, I never wanted to be a musician or performer, however, music has been the path that led me to discover my true potential.

After school, I would come home to listen to the songs I liked the most and then write them down in a small sketchbook. I remember the brand very well: Caribe. It had on its cover the image of an Indian in a corner, enclosed in a circle, the rest of the space was filled with blue and white hexagons. I believe that this brand is no longer on the market or simply they no longer have that model that now they would call *retro*.

I listened to the songs of rock groups or pop music soloists who dragged thousands of fans to their concerts, where they cried, despaired and seemed to be possessed by a magical energy that pulsed every event they offered. The likes of Donna Summer, Diana Ross, Michael Jackson, ABBA, Queen, Led Zeppelin, Pink Floyd, Bee Gees, Eric

21

Carmen, Bruce Springsteen, Hall & Oates, Earth, Wind & Fire, were my favorite artists, the ones I listened to the most.

That was in the late seventies and early eighties, as a teenager, when I began to immerse myself in this musical world. I thank God deeply for having been a young man of that era and not of the current one. It's not that this one is bad, not at all, the tools of today make everyone's life much easier, and I think that's what I don't like, that there are so many tools and very little struggle. It is my perception, a very personal way of reasoning. The truth is that destiny does not make mistakes and puts everyone where they belong and the eighties was the ideal decade for me, it's as simple as that.

At that age, what I always liked about music was not precisely its chords, instruments or musical equipment, much less the beautiful voices of those who performed each song. What really moved my soul was writing and reviewing what was going on in the entertainment world at that time.

When I was in high school, or *high school,* as it is called in the United States, at about the age of sixteen I bought the magazines of the artistic world of the time. I did it because I wanted to follow the careers of the musical and television idols of the time.

One of those special days you have in life, when you get crazy about an idea that doesn't leave you alone and that starts going round and round in your head and, by the way, doesn't allow you to concentrate on anything else, I decided to introduce myself as a writer at the Dearmas Block, the center of the most prestigious Venezuelan and foreign show business newspapers and magazines. It was the place in Venezuela where most of the reports from the world of music and show business were published. The magazines *Venezuela Farándula, Ronda, Variedades, Momento, Bohemia,* and the newspapers *Meridiano and*

2001 were part of this information complex.

Now, I was confident in my pulse, but I didn't know the magnitude of the surprise that awaited me....

MY FUTURE WITH A "TIN MARÍN".

It was then that I decided to take the risk and apply to the Dearmas Block as a writer. Something inside me urged me to go, I knew I had a lot of potential for writing. I was good at writing entertainment news. I followed in detail the lives of most of the celebrities of the time, their successes, their heartaches, their projects. So, without giving the matter much thought, I made up an appointment with the editorial management of the famed editorial block.

It was a crazy thing to do, because I was so confident in myself, in my talent, in my way of writing, that I never had any fear. On the contrary, I knew that I had to do it, that I had to take the risk and, without hesitation, I went for the adventure. What did I have to lose? Nothing, but I had a lot to gain.

Since I didn't know anyone, I went around the *lobby* area until I made up my mind. In the address of the magazines, the names of two directors appeared: Gloria Fuentes and Rosana Ordóñez.

When I approached the reception desk, I told the lady at the front desk that I had an appointment at the editorial office. She immediately asked me with whom I had the appointment scheduled. Like every boy, I got that scare that hits you in the stomach when you think you are doing something wrong, and like every little boy, I solved the problem the way I had as a child, with the sorting song, "tin marín"; similar to the American children's song "Eeny, meeny, miny, moe".

De tin marín de dos pingüé*,
Cúcara, mácara, títere fue,
Yo no fui, fue Teté,
Pégale, pégale, al quien fue.

Then, respecting the result, I told the lady that my appointment was scheduled with the director Rosana Ordóñez. They called her office and asked her if she had an appointment with Carlos Camargo.

At this point my palms began to sweat and I crossed my fingers. Ordóñez's response was that if I said I had an appointment with him, then so be it. What happened was that she did not remember the appointment. An appointment that had never been scheduled because it did not exist.

I went up to his office on the seventh floor. The elevator ride was slow, which filled me with anxiety and nerves. I entered his office and introduced myself. To his surprise, I was wearing my school uniform, I was just out of school. At that time I was in my fifth and last year of high school. She immediately asked me if I really had an appointment with her.

A PROOF CONVINCING

There are two things for which I will always be grateful for that first interview: my courage for the initiative to venture into that meeting and Rosana's absent-mindedness. Later a very good friend of mine. Now shining in the sky.

After the formal presentation, she got up from her chair and left her office for a moment, leaving me there alone for more than an hour. On her return she apologized to me, excusing herself because she had so much to do. The publishing house was in final editing for the launch of its magazines and there were many details to work out.

I began to talk like never before, I said everything I was capable of doing, I talked about the enormous desire I had to write, about what I had been doing since I was a child. I told her about the life of famous singers and artists of the time, in short, I left my whole brain on her desk. In fact, I didn't even let her speak, I had to unleash my entire arsenal without giving her time to respond.

It was twenty minutes of exposition. When I finished, she was stunned, perhaps disoriented, until she asked me if I wanted to study journalism or something similar. At that moment, with my eyes wide open and my heart pounding, I answered that I had gone to work immediately as a writer. It was an immense need that was out of my control and that I had to exploit.

Obviously, Rosana thought it was a bit crazy that a pubescent boy of my age would ask her to work as a writer for one of the most respected publishers in the country. She, very kindly to get out of the way, asked me to bring her a sample of my talent. I had to submit it the following week and I, not being short or lazy, left happier than a boy w th a new toy and began to write what I considered the best of my editions at that time.

The following week, without fail, I went to her office again. This time she was sure of my appointment and received me kindly. She took my writing, read it slowly, in detail, until she finished and told me that it seemed impossible to her that I, being just a boy, could write in such a way.

Of course I told him that I did indeed write like that. I told her that I had written the press release, that I had unleashed all my talent in writing it, and that I, only I, was the author of the issue. Rosana, to clear her doubts, told me the following:

"Since you claim to be your author, I'll leave you a task. Sit there, next to my desk and write a press release about this article, something short, fill this page for me."

EXAMPLE OF A PASTERN

(25 LINES) WEAPONS BLOCK

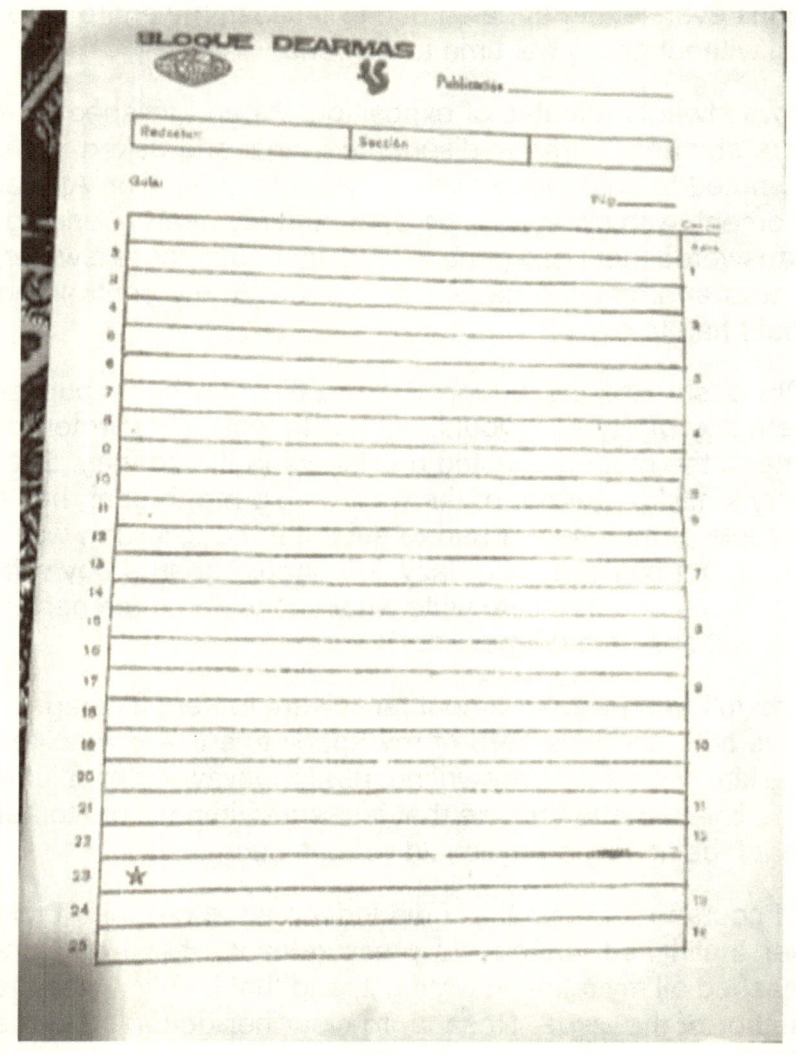

I did not know what a sheet of paper was. She gave me a sheet of paper with twenty-five printed lines and explained to me what a sheet of paper was, she told me to fill out the sheet with the information she was going to give me.

In accordance with his request, I took the typewriter, my sheet of paper and began to write a press release *on* Franco de Vita *on the spot*, which had to surpass the previous one. First, because I needed to clear up any doubts about it and, second, because I wanted to show him that I was ready for action.

Rosana, when she finished reading it, said to me:

"Wow, I love it! What do you want, to write about politics or about shows? If you want to write about politics, I'll leave you some material for you to publish a report on presidential candidate José Vicente Rangel, because I have a magazine called *Momento,* where you can write anything, but in *Bohemia it*'s more complicated."

My response, to my greatest joy, was that I could write whatever he asked me to write. He told me to write what I honestly wanted to write and to deliver it to him the following week.

Thus I began my work in the Dearmas Block, with a column in the magazine *Momento* which I called "Ecos de estrellas", and later Rosana Ordóñez would change the name to "Estrellas al día", small informative notes on the artists of the moment, such as Franco de Vita, Yordano, Madonna, Steve Wonder, George Michael, Prince, Michael Jackson, among others.

After about three months, they called me to talk to me. They told me they wanted to hire me at once. So I started as a staff writer for *Momento* and *Bohemia* magazines, and then I went on to write for thirteen other magazines.

This is how my story in the world of writing and social communication began, with just seventeen years old and an unplanned interview, driven by my passion for writing. Today I have thirty-seven years of activities with them, besides working for other media inside and outside Venezuela.

MY START AS EDITOR

After I was accepted as a permanent editor in the Dearmas Block, I had to deal with my world: finish my last year in high school, of which I have a good story to tell, organize my musical shows, because by then I had a mini-venue called *Music Pop*, and attend to my job as programming assistant for Radio Metropolitana, the first AM stereo station in the city of Los Teques, my city of residence. As you can see, at the age of seventeen I had a busy life, with a lot to do and a lot to discover.

By that year, the minitek wars were the ultimate musical thrill for a youngster like me to attend. In fact, there were big events featuring the best miniteks in the country: Sandy Lane, Betelgeuse, Excalibur, New York New York, among others.

I attended almost all the events to enjoy all the musical power and the play of lights that overflowed in the presentations. Of course, I also showed off my talents as a *disc jockey*, which served as a springboard for me to join the aforementioned radio station.

Among the events and musical presentations of national and foreign artists, which I attended regularly out of conviction and pleasure, I met a journalist named Héctor Bermúdez, entertainment editor of the magazine *Ronda* del Bloque Dearmas.

He was a journalist who was more into politics and opinion, and I was a young editor who loved show business. We both worked for the same company, but in environments contrary to our passions.

On one occasion, the two editors of the editorial magazines noticed what each of us was passionate about. Héctor worked with Gloria Fuentes, director of the entertainment magazines, and I worked with Rosana Ordóñez, director of the opinion and political magazines. So, both decided to make a kind of barter and place each editor in his or her ideal work environment. Since then, I have been an active entertainment editor.

Little by little I became known in the media. Many readers followed my reports in the magazines *Momento, Ronda* and *Venezuela Farándula,* and I continued with my ant-like work in the different events presented in Caracas and neighboring cities, besides becoming popular in Los Teques, the city where I lived. That's how I became friends with the production manager of Radio Metropolitana, AM Stereo, who, upon seeing my musical talent, took me to the radio station so that I could have my own mix show, one that was broadcasted at night.

My good taste in music selection helped me to be appointed assistant to the production management, and that's how that small and nascent radio station became the owner of the city's *rating.*

MY ENDEAVOR TO GRADUATE *SUMMA CUM LAUDE*

I was only a few months away from finishing my high school and I wanted to graduate with honors. Despite the multiple responsibilities I had to take care of, my studies were never relegated to a secondary plane. In fact, my greatest motivation was to graduate with honors to enter a good university, this is what is always said in the homes of all Venezuelans. Studying at a prestigious university was a "guarantee" of professional success.

I had a good academic record in all subjects. My dream of graduating with the highest laurels was about to be fulfilled, it had been a phenomenal year in which all my dreams materialized. But the day came to take the Chemistry exam. If I passed with twenty points, which was the maximum grade, I was assured of my place on the honor roll. There was only one small drawback: the teacher.

I was one of those professors who did not like to give a twenty, I don't know if it was because he was a crafty one, to maintain that profile of "the strictest", or "the most demanding", or because he was one of those who thought that only the author of the chemistry book and the professor deserved a twenty, the rest had to be satisfied with a nineteen, at the most.

Since I am not one to settle for what is given to me, but one to demand what I rightfully deserve, I was ready to fight for my twenty. I was already mentally prepared.

I had studied hard in the days leading up to the exam. I was sure I would get every item on the test right. I had no doubt that I would get the highest score, I knew everything, absolutely everything.

The day of the exam came and with it, my biggest disappointment. I did not get a twenty on my exam, I had scored nineteen points. With a great feeling of anger, because it was nothing more than that, I approached the professor's desk and had an impasse.

I had a serious discussion. I knew beforehand his unhealthy habit of not giving the grade deserved to those who were so dedicated to study. It was my anger that the most dedicated students were the ones who were the most harassed, while those, the careless ones, often received higher grades than they really deserved.

That impasse and complaint brought consequences. I failed the exam, they sent me for repairs and I was almost expelled from school. For a moment my dream of graduating with honors vanished. However, in the make-up test I got the twenty and, consequently, my greatest desire.

MY GREATEST SCHOOL: MY WORKPLACE

Once I finished high school, the biggest challenge was to get into the university. In Venezuela, all students in their last year of high school take the university admission test, formerly known as the CNU test, now known as OPSU. It is a test that measures your knowledge and your professional vocation. It gives you the opportunity to choose three careers to study in public universities, something that all high school students seek, because private universities have always been very expensive in my country.

As a matter of course, I selected Social Communication as my first choice, and Modern Languages as my second choice. When the results were published, I noticed that I was not admitted to study my first choice, but that I had secured a place to study Modern Languages. It was not the career I preferred, but I thought that, by taking a couple of semesters, I was free to ask for a change of major. But no, my application was never approved, which made it very difficult to continue my studies at the Universidad Central de Venezuela, the best university in the country.

My boss, Rosana Ordóñez, and Don Armando de Armas, helped me to get into another good university, only this one is private: the Universidad Católica Andrés Bello. With much excitement, and thanking the support of my superiors and classmates, I began my studies at UCAB.

The classes, in my opinion, were boring. I did not learn much; on the contrary, they learned from me. I was already working in journalism and everything they taught in the classroom I had already learned from my classmates and superiors. Every time the teacher assigned a task, I had it done beforehand for my work or I delivered it the next day in a printed publication in a magazine or a newspaper.

I served as a monitor for the teachers. While they taught the class for a week or so, I learned it in a matter of hours on the job. I had the best professionals in the country working with me, the best teachers I had in my life.

Soon after, due to work issues and lack of motivation, I froze my career, I continued learning in the field, where you really "beat the odds", as we say in our popular slang. After two years I resumed my studies and graduated as a Social Communicator in Print Media, a degree that I received and kept I don't know where, because my best university has simply been my work.

FROM EDITORIAL WRITER TO ARTISTS' PRESS REP-RESENTATIVE

My biggest launching pad in the news media has undoubtedly been my home, the Dearmas Block. This has been more than my workplace, my home, my family and my greatest blessing. Here I started and continue to grow as a professional.

Once I started as an editor, after almost two years of work, I was promoted to executive producer. My job there was to put together the content of different magazines. I was responsible for editing the content of the magazines *Variedades, Ideas Festivas, Moda,* supporting the content of *Fama, Ronda, Venezuela Farándula, Súper Pop, Bravísimo, De Todo,* and the special editions, among others. I held this position for seventeen years.

In the meantime, I covered vacancies, vacations of some journalist and even reports in *Diario 2001;* then together with my boss, Gloria Fuentes, we created the do-it-yourself magazines called *Apparel* and *Dress,* magazines of sewing patterns and guidance for fashion designers. I also created *Bonita* magazine, which was my favorite in the Dearmas Block, for quinceañeras and teenagers. I had 100% Venezuelan material, with my own images of Venezuelan models and actresses, then I started to create my own original image bank for the Dearmas Block. Thanks to my management, the people of the newspaper *El Nacional* hired me to take the Sunday insert *Feriado* to magazine format, thanks to the journalists Aquilino José Mata and Virgilio Fernández. I spent six years with them in charge of the project as editorial producer.

My fame as a producer was increasing and I was making fun of being one of the best in the area. In *2001* I started working in a show business column called *Camargonotas, a* column that is still active today, after twenty years.

Then, I opened a *freelance* company for the promotion of record labels. With it I offered my services to promote the records of different artists. Rafael Fuentes Jr., assistant director of Bloque Dearmas, was also working at that time with a label called Magic Records, leader in the presentation of colored records, widely used in *remix* music. The main clients of the colored format were the *disco music* or eighties music performers. Rafael asked me to promote the material in the different radio stations and media of the city so that they would publish the new musical themes reproduced in the chromatic copies.

With this work I cultivated my fame as a promoter, which opened doors for me at Fama Récords, Pepe Récords, Manoca Récords, Top Hits Récords and, of course, Magic Récords.

During the eighties Venezuela was the springboard for many artists to enter the Latin American market. If they hit in Venezuela, they were guaranteed success in Latin America. Artists such as Ricky Martin, Emmanuel, Miguel Bosé, Chayanne, Rocío Jurado, Rocío Dúrcal, Juan Gabriel, Maná, Luis Miguel, used the media platform in the oil country to project their careers.

Much later, representatives of various artists began to hire me as promoter and press officer in Venezuela. Olga Tañón was one of them. They joined, the musical Violeta,

Romeo Santos, J. Balvin, Vivian Sleiman, among many others. Press officer for concerts with companies such as Only Ticket Eventos, Emporio Group and the presentations of Vicente Fernández, Juan Gabriel and the group Maná of businessman José Luis Parra. This in alliance with Carmen Montoya.

In one of those twists of fate, Oscar D'León's *manager*, Oswaldo Ponte, one day when he went to the Sonográfica record label, asked for Olga Tañón's press officer. He began to like the work I was doing in the media and wanted to meet me. The label gave him my contact number, and when I least expected it, I received a call from him.

-How come you're only Olga Tañón's press officer? What kind of bullshit is that? No sir, you also have to be Oscar D'León's press officer. You're already hired, I like what you do. Let's get together.

I responded that it would be an honor for me to be his press representative and after eighteen years, I continue to work with the "Sonero del mundo", as this great artist is known. The list includes Aguasanta Erminy, Chiquinquirá Delgado, Porfi Baloa, Luis Silva, Rummy Olivo, among many others.

THE CARD THAT KILLED THE LOUSE IN THE HEAD

The people from the Fifth Miss Venezuela called me to serve as a *scout* for aspiring models for the beauty pageant. Osmel sent me to the universities for the *scouting* process. So, following his instructions, I visited the faculties of Social Communication, Dentistry and Law of the famous universities of the capital and invited them to participate as models for commercials for Mariela Centeno's agency Mariela New Style.

Once they arrived at the agency, we gave them the news that they were pre-selected for the Miss Venezuela pageant. Among those pre-candidates was Eva Lisa Ljung, a beautiful girl of Swedish origin who arrived in the country when she was only four years old, and was later naturalized by her parents.

She and I almost immediately formed a beautiful friendship. Our professional relationship was very fluid and her confidence in me was absolute. In 1991 this beautiful model won the Miss Venezuela pageant, of course, it was a *boom* and her detractors began to build a conspiracy to make her give up the crown because of her Swedish origin.

As soon as I received the news, I contacted her and asked for her laminated ID card and went to the Dearmas Block and with all the acceleration that the process deserved, we gave, what they call in the journalistic jargon, "the tubazo". I was in charge of making the press release and publishing the image of the identity card that verified the nationality of the young beauty queen.

The headline in the media was: "Eva Lisa Ljung, more Venezuelan than arepa", and with that proof I put an end to the confused matrix of information that some media had published.

After this work, Osmel Sousa and I became close friends, so much so that I was his promoter in several projects that he executed, hand in hand with Gabriel Ramos, such as the line for hair care in partnership with Rembrandt Cosmetics, and the line of hairdressers *By Osmel*. The image of the hairdresser's model was the young former Miss Venezuela and model Mariángel Ruiz and, in some cases, he launched a promotion of hair washing by models of the Míster Venezuela, as a marketing strategy.

THE POWER OF VISUALIZATION

Everything I have told you up to this point has not been a

mere work of chance and much less the capricious game of destiny. Everything that has happened to me and will continue to happen is the work and art of God and the power of visualization, of hard work to consolidate it. I am a dreamer, but I do it awake, with my feet firmly on the ground and my eyes on the future.

Visualization "is the light that goes through a passage of reflections and returns to itself: it is a hand that invents itself, an eye that looks at itself in its inventions. Light is time that thinks itself," said the great Mexican poet Octavio Paz.

As a child I envisioned myself as a writer, and so it was. As a teenager I visualized myself in the world of music, as a producer, promoter and editor, and so it was. I was a *disc jockey,* production assistant and promoter of several musical artists in the world of radio and show business.

I have visualized myself as my own boss, and now I work for myself, in my schedule, in my disposition and I live my life at my pleasure, without stopping producing, fulfilling my commitments and without stopping dreaming, because I continue to devise my future, carved to perfection, because the world and technology advance and you have to keep up with them, you have to innovate and set the pace, if you stand still you lose, and life is too beautiful to lose.

What was it? Is it or isn't it? The Marcos Vargas of the loud cry in the face of danger, of the heart inflamed before the sovereign force, once again as before, joyful and confident. The wind! The roaring hurricane that swept through the foliage, tearing apart the branches, the immense garrison of the hooting among the cordage of the lianas, the shrill whistle on the edge of the leaf, the impetuous snort against the creeping bush, the scream of terror that strangled the throat of the ravine, the mad, blind and clumsy race, the exit sought and not found, the furious revolt, the thunderstorm again...

Fragment of Canaima,
Romulo Gallegos

CHAPTER 2

THE VALUES THAT HAVE MARKED MY LIFE

The Venezuelan family, in general, respects and defends the moral and ethical values imposed by society and religion. Sadly, at present, these values have suffered a degenerative crisis that is better not to talk about in this book; we leave that subject to the experts in sociology and anthropology.

Although my life has been marked by certain ethical and moral qualities that I have learned from my family, school and work environment, the most important values, those that have made me what I am today, are the values that I have learned by intuition, empiricism or practicality.

The selfless honesty, the competent responsibility, the consecrated commitment, the passion for doing things, the brilliant cunning, the spirited daring and the impetuous impulse of risk are values and virtues that characterize me. Thanks to them I have maintained my focus and persistence in the consolidation of the goals I have set for myself and, like that intrepid Marcos Vargas in *Canaima*, I go into my jungle and face life with that bravery or courage that, as a free spirit, runs through its thicket without being devoured by it, which could explain part of my professional success.

I advise everyone to take risks, to venture. In my particular case, the comfort zone has not been and will not be a stable zone for me, because I love to go beyond it. I like to know that my own stable space is the one that does not limit me to stay in a certain place, but rather, I work to make that zone as wide as I can, that really brings me comfort.

COMMITMENT: MY DEDICATION TO ONE HUNDRED PERCENT

Commitment implies one hundred percent dedication, it is an acquired responsibility that fully demonstrates the kind of person you really are.

For most, the value of commitment is subject to the professional, work or academic field, and it is not so, it is in everything you have to do and that, without realizing it, builds your image.

If you are going to clean your house, for example, you must be aware that the work must be exhaustive, deep and that it deserves your full attention. Otherwise, you will spend all day cleaning and you will realize that you did not clean everything, which will lead you to make a serious mistake, that of making excuses that will easily justify your distractions. For example, that the house is too big to be cleaned by only one person, that it was too dirty, that there were too many dishes to move, among other things.

I give myself completely to each of my commitments and it is very difficult for me to give them up, from cleaning my house to writing, the activity that allows me to have the quality of life I have. As a piece of advice, when you commit yourself to something, give yourself with all your love and you will see that you will enjoy it and that it will turn out better than you expected.

From my perception, commitment is a state of mind, because every task, work or activity requires and deserves total attention, no matter how banal or simple it may seem. This is how I guarantee the quality of my work, because I am a professional who is fully committed, which demonstrates my competence in the tasks I take on, whether I know the subject or not, because I have taken on the challenge, I research, investigate and look for the necessary tools to fulfill it.

An example of the value I place on my commitments is the following: before the pandemic, I was traveling with Oscar D'León on his annual tour around the world. At the airport, while waiting to board the plane, I would write a press release on my phone to be published in one of the news portals I work for, such as *Camargonotas* of *Diario 2001* or *Camargo Notas* of *El Venezolano de Miami*, Noti-

ExpressColor, among others.

Then, during the flight, I would write more press releases on my news blog. Upon arrival in Milan, one of the destination cities, during the waiting time for baggage delivery, or while waiting for transportation, I would deliver to the different media all the press releases I had done during the flight.

I do not stop working, I am a man who makes the most of my working time, my commitments with all the news agencies I work for have been acquired for many years, time that speaks for itself of the fruit of my one hundred percent dedication.

TIME: A NON-RENEWABLE RESOURCE

We should not take the value of commitment as a factor that is anchored to time, if so, you will become its slave. I have heard of many people who ask to have a forty-eight hour day to do everything they have to do in twenty-four hours, because it already seems insufficient to them, that is the common denominator.

The problem lies in the time invested in things that do not require it, that is, procrastinating by not calibrating in the mind a list of really important priorities that can provide quality of life and happiness.

There are many people who waste hours sending an email or elaborating a two-page report. If they would focus on each task without being so scattered, they would reduce considerably the execution time and could do other things, that is called profit. There are things that do require time investment and are those that allow you to grow and live, the rest are just things that do not deserve such a precious resource.

I work to get things done as soon as possible and from

very early in the morning, I am one of those who under-stand the saying: "The early bird catches the worm". I do it because I want to have as much free time as possible to enjoy activities that make me happy, that is quality of life.

Time should not be underestimated by putting off until later what you can do immediately, by trusting in your abilities to do things. The passage of time is something that affects all aspects of life, because, unlike money and other material goods, time spent is irretrievable, it does not come back to us nor can we buy it, it is the most precious thing we can have and we must treat it fairly and not waste it. Definitely, time is a non-renewable resource.

BOLDNESS: MY GREATEST VIRTUE

To make good use of time we must be daring. There are things that cannot wait, there are decisions that require promptness, there is a reason why it is said that time is money. In my case, boldness is my best friend and taking risks in difficult situations is my greatest virtue.

I'll give you an example, my English is not good and every time I communicate with an English speaker, I say be-forehand: "*So sorry, my English is not good*". Still, I write articles in English. Language is not an impediment to ac-complish my work, I use the tools I have available, such as translators, I rely on friends who speak the language, I ask them if my article is well written and they kindly tell me if it is or not.

Many times I have had problems with some *apostrophes* or some misused *have's* that I have been corrected. This hasn't stopped me even though I can't write in English be-cause I don't speak it well.

People will think: "Wow! Carlos writes in English," not knowing that I actually write it in Spanish. Then, I evaluate how I can do it in English, understanding that it is grammatically different from Spanish. That is having determination, being bold, taking risks and being a daredevil, a daredevil who plays with the language, as many have told me.

That is my essence, my determination and courage to do my best, which is then reflected in the quality of my work that has been published in media such as *Los Angeles Wire, The San Francisco Post, The Times, Miami Wires, US News* and affiliates of FOX, NBC, CBS, among more than 50 American media.

There is an anecdote, one of many I have from the Dearmas Block, that surprised many, especially Marita Capote, a Venezuelan singer and actress who shone during the last decades of the last century.

In a section I used to write called *Cara a cara a cara of Venezuela Farándula* magazine, I invited her to an interview with her sister Tatiana Capote, literally face to face. Tatiana, when she started talking, noticed that I didn't have a tape recorder and told me that she didn't want me to write down words that I hadn't said. Of course, I told her that was not going to happen.

As she was still a little hesitant, she told me that if I wrote in the section everything she told me, as is, she would give me lunch.

She did not count on one of my greatest talents, if it can be called that way, which was an incredible mastery of mnemonics. In my student years, both in elementary school and high school, even in college, mnemonics was the resource I used the most to study, therefore, I developed an incredible mastery of its use, which has allowed me to memorize to the letter almost everything I read or hear. So I applied it in that interview and memorized every word Marita and Tatiana told me.

When the publication came out, Tatiana could not believe it, she had read in the section every word I had said, without any modification, and it was then that my courage and my risk allowed me to have a free lunch in her company, laughing and talking about a fact so impressive for her and so regular for me.

SET PRIORITIES: MY METHOD OF WORK

I am not a man of methods, I think that mnemonics is the only technique I usually use, which allows me to organize in my mind everything I have to do. Some people use diaries, I don't. Agendas for me are for writing from January 1 to January 15 "BEACH!", the rest of the pages are kept blank, for that I use a notebook.

In this sense, I'm sure you're wondering what method or strategy I use to comply with all the media I work for, and that is to establish an order of priorities. To achieve this, I simply turn to official sources that are promoters of events of impact in the world of show business and entertainment and, depending on their impact, I write a press release to send to the different publication media.

YOU HAVE TO LOVE WHAT YOU DO

There is nothing more rewarding and pleasurable than doing something you love and enjoy doing. Working on things you don't love gradually sours your mood, steals your energy and with it your happiness.

I can understand that many people work because they have not had the joy of doing what they are passionate about, because life has been unfair, because of fate, in short, because of things that they cannot explain, but if you are one of them, look for a reason to learn from what you do, discover in your work what can be useful for your life, you will see that you will immediately feel joy and you will start to enjoy your work.

Every single thing we do leaves a teaching, a lesson. There is nothing we do that we cannot take advantage of. I am an advocate and promoter of this premise and I tell you that happiness has always been and will always be in you, it cannot be found anywhere else. Look for it within yourself and enjoy it, work with joy and you will see better results, besides having a better mood, which will be appreciated by those around you.

Once, the press representative of a very famous reggaeton artist called me to be part of his team of promoters of his musical career. I politely declined the offer, which they wanted to counter with a good offer of a fee, and again I declined.

I don't work in something I am not passionate about. That musical genre for me, with respect to its representatives, is not music and that is why I did not accept. I was not going to feel comfortable promoting songs that I don't really like and in order not to break my peace of mind, I preferred to stop earning that money if it was going to detract from my happiness.

CREATIVITY AND INNOVATION: MY GREATEST RE-SOURCE

Instinct and logic have been my compass, with them I have succeeded, so to speak, in the bet for success, in several projects that I have proposed.

In this environment, if you are not dynamic, creative and innovative, little by little the road becomes uphill and you end up on the sidelines, watching others who are.

In my case, innovation is a characteristic of my own, which makes me a great visionary in my field. With it, I have achieved great feats that have marked a milestone in my career. About seven years ago, I started to hear and read about *streaming.* Within my environment, no one knew about it.

Little by little I started researching and reading in some Spanish magazines such as *Muy Interesante, Interview and Selecciones*, or the German magazine *Stern,* very well developed articles on the point in question.

I went to a friend of mine, Alepuro, who is very good with technology and asked him to explain more about it. Of course, he kindly gave me a master class on the transmission of multimedia content over the Internet, without the need to download it. Immediately, I remembered that Oscar D'León was about to launch his book to the market and I started to prepare a press conference on *streaming.* And that was how I achieved the first press conference with the use of this emerging technology.

Media from Japan, France, Spain, Dominican Republic and other countries, intervened in the transmission, thanks to the digital platform of the newspaper *El Nacional.* It was a transmission from the Eurobuilding Hotel, and it is now that everyone transmits via *streaming,* something I already did in 2014.

As I do not stay quiet, I have already started to investigate the benefits offered by NFC *(Near Field Communication)* technology, to use it as a means of dissemination of my content page in the different magazines I manage or the press columns I write for different newspapers.

By simply pasting my phone number to the interested contact, I pass on the digital material that I offer. In short, I am and always will be an innovator, because, with technology you have to be at least one step ahead to stay active in this field of work. In addition, I am researching to have knowledge to make a musical show or launch in virtual reality.

THE MASTER'S EYE FATTENS THE CATTLE

Teamwork is one of my greatest strengths. I am not a superhuman who is able to do everything, although I am very competent in the things I do. However, there are times when I have to be honest with myself and accept that there are experts in some areas that I handle that can bring more quality to each of my jobs.

That is why I was able to put together a team of experts in their areas, who help me develop my projects, but before the material goes to publication, I review and approve it, if I find something that does not convince me, I send it back and ask them to improve it. Sometimes I tend to be very severe, it is due to how rigorous I am in my requests, I like perfection and if someone does not give it to me, then they cannot work in my team.

That is why I have achieved success in each of my projects, because I get fully involved, supervise, contribute, demand, teach and learn from each of my collaborators. If I see something in a magazine that can give a *plus* to my publications, I apply it and set my own style. I believe in teamwork, as long as they follow instructions of excellence.

FOCUS: THE BEST COMPASS THAT MARKS MY NORTH

I enjoy everything I do, to achieve it I keep the focus; it is not something easy to do, but you can cultivate it, you can learn to use it. To achieve it you have to avoid distractions, which I do not accept, I go to the point, I fix my gaze on my north, my thoughts and my senses for the development of my work.

I invest my energy and ten minutes of my time to plan and

visualize what I want to do. I am a shrewd man by nature and I love challenges and, as I said before, if I don't know the subject, I take the risks, I prepare myself to feel capable to achieve my goals.

I was recently asked if I was able to milk a cow. As I currently live in a cattle area, it is very common to see people milking. I didn't refuse to do it, I immediately said that I had seen them take the udder, squeeze it and give it a little tug downwards to let the spurt come out.

Some of them laughed and explained the technique to me a little bit. I immediately started milking and today I can tell you that I am almost a professional, every time I see a cow I want to milk it, it is things like that add happiness to my life.

I am a man very confident of my strengths and capabilities, that drives me to do things, I apply my five senses to everything I do and I have all my attention to learn and do very well what I set out to do.

ADAPTABILITY: THE NATURE OF THE SUCCESSFUL MAN

Human beings, by nature, are able to adapt to any climate, geography, space or technological development, however, it must be accepted that there are people who have developed this condition better than others.

I regularly like to change the environment in which I operate. And it is those changes that make it more comfortable for me. I am not a man to put buts to changes, on the contrary, I love challenges, new things, even difficulties, that keeps me entertained, which gives me excitement.

When I lived in Orlando, Florida, I occupied a five-bedroom house for a year. I was the only tenant in that space and I adapted to it. I had a game room, a TV room, my bedroom, a work space and a reading space. Since it was close to the theme parks, I went there every day.

The actors in the shows already knew me and I collaborated with them as a photographer when tourists asked for a photo with them. During that time, that was my comfort zone and when I stopped feeling comfortable, I moved to Miami, to a studio apartment, and now, uncomfortable in that place, not because of the space, but because of how routine it became, I bought a *motor home,* in which I now travel all over the United States, comfortable in this small space where I have everything I need.

Material things don't tie me down, I don't live to show opulence, I live to be happy. Social status doesn't worry me, I don't care if I have a simple watch made in China or a Rolex; in fact, I have a Louis Vuitton that I don't use, the purpose of both devices is to mark the time, and since I don't work for time, but time works for me, I will be less likely to be seen wearing one of them, because time for me is only poetry and a watch its prodigal slave.

The watch

continued to cut off time

with its small saw.

As in a forest

go to

wood fragments,

tiny drops, pieces

of branches or nests,

without changing the silence,

without the cool darkness ending,

so

kept the clock ticking

from your invisible hand,

time, time,

and fell

minutes as leaves,

broken time fibers,

small black feathers.

Excerpt from *Ode to a clock at night*
Pablo Neruda

Before the dream (or the terror) weave

mythologies and cosmogonies,

before time was coined in days,

the sea, the always sea, already was and was.

Who is the sea?

Who is that violent

and ancient being that gnaws at the pillars

of the earth and it is one and many seas

and abyss and glow and chance and wind?

Whoever looks at it sees it for the first time, always.

With the amazement that things

elemental leaves, the beautiful

evenings, the moon, the fire of a bonfire.

Who is the sea, who am I?

I will know the day

ulterior that follows the agony.

Poem *The Sea*

Jorge Luis Borges

CHAPTER 3

MY WAY

56

Panama City, Florida, is my place of escape. Contact with the sea is my favorite place to recharge my batteries. I love to be on its beaches, enjoy the sunrises and sunsets that the sea coast offers me.

I love to witness a silent romance between the crystalline waters and the coastline. The waves, exhausted by their intrepid journey to the kingdom of Poseidon, love to reach its shore and delivered, kiss the sand of their beloved beach, a furtive kiss, invisible under its layer of foam.

Every time I want to see a beach sunrise I move to this, my personal paradise. Here I feel peace, serenity. My soul detaches itself from my being and takes over the environment. The sea breeze, perfumed by the saltpeter, becomes my breath of life and the immensity that is drawn on the horizon, unconquerable and impetuous, envelops me in an instant.

The spectacle in every dawn begins before dawn. I prepare myself from the blue hour, the point at which the celestial vault begins to shed its nocturnal veil. Gradually, the flickering frost of its mantle disappears and an amethyst dye begins to distill, announcing the arrival of the sun king.

Then, with a magical touch, the cosmographic canvas displays a range of colors that start from a faint indigo to a golden range, giving off all its shades. Finally, a beautiful grapefruit rises from behind the thin line of the horizon.

All this spectacle that God gives us, I receive it with open arms, surrendered to his infinite love. I perceive it with my bare feet on the albino sand that sinks with every step I take and that imprints each of my footprints. I observe that clear sky until the sun's rays whiten.

Once the show is over, I walk along the beach listening to their tune, lost songs of mermaids that break with the waves and then leave, riding the untamed wind, turned into whistles blown by the sea.

This magnificent work of the Creator allows me to free myself from everything that disturbs the world and that can affect me emotionally, mentally and spiritually. It is not an isolation mechanism, I call it, rather, an energetic recharge.

I am the director of a news portal called *Noti-America.* I receive daily news of all kinds and some, by their nature, are disturbing. They make me think about the vulnerability of the human mind, so I protect myself and avoid being affected, recharge my energies and feel renewed.

My lifestyle aims at spiritual enrichment, emotional well-being and everything that brings me happiness. I don't let myself be impacted by the news that comes into my hands, I just transmit and release it, otherwise, I would have a lifestyle opposite to the one I live, one that I don't want to lose.

Just as I enjoy the pleasure of the sun, the sea and the sand, I enjoy every landscape that nature gives me and, why not, the emblematic places that humanity has left through time. I enjoy one day at a time, without projections, without planning, without expectations, I just go out and let God be my guide.

THE ENCOUNTER WITH MY CURRENT LIFESTYLE

There are many people who are tireless at work. They spend every day, from sunrise to sunset, immersed in tasks and chores, in projects and papers, but they do not enjoy the gift of life, those little things that make you feel really alive.

From my point of view, it is a very personal appreciation, I can say that the richest people in the world only have money, properties and accumulation of material goods, but they are not happy. As an entertainment journalist, I know the lives of these people by heart. I follow every step they take because my job requires it, I know their successes and their failures, their marriages and then their quick separations.

I don't want to have that kind of life no matter how much money I can accumulate. I am a human being who has learned to live without being tied to money. If I have an arepita in the morning and an arepita at night, I am done.

To acquire this lifestyle I had to leave aside, by conviction and by lessons, the material attachment. I understood that I can live happily without having to earn a large salary, of course, without ceasing to understand that money is necessary, because it complements my tastes, but without being attached to its whims and vanities, it is only a vehicle that allows me to get what I really need.

There are people who waste the most valuable resource, time, in a job that demands unnecessarily many hours, in order to accumulate money that they will spend on the purchase of something that will not bring them happiness.

I understood that I could do the same work I was doing in eight hours in one hour and I was free for the rest of the day. I did it once, then I did it a second time and realized that I gained quality time for myself. I knew then what I had to do: work in as little time as possible with the same quality, but without being scattered or wasteful of minutes, and earn the same money and more hours for myself, to do what I wanted.

So it was that this rhythm of work became my lifestyle. I work for a while, well focused and well delivered, without distractions, without waste of time, I get the same result, a quality work, well completed, in the shortest time possible, to have for me the most amount of freedom and invest in my professional growth, in my enjoyment and recreation, this is quality of life.

People who know me tell me that they want to live life like me, but what's stopping them? Everyone can work and enjoy that quality time that allows them to lead a healthy, pleasurable life, able to enjoy nature, landscapes and even to get to know other countries or do other activities.

I can understand that there are people who work in an office, because their work style and work rhythm requires it, a rhythm very different from mine, because I can work with a phone or a *laptop* in any corner of the world, as long as I have electricity and Internet, but many of those "office" people choose to continue their work at home.

My brother is a doctor. He has hard days where he spends entire days on call at a hospital. In the morning he sees his patients, most of the time, in his office. Other times he sees patients in the operating room, surgery, triage or hospitalization. At the end of his day, he leaves the hospital, carries his stethoscope on his shoulders and goes home.

At home, with his family, he takes calls from his patients and gives them telephone consultations. He can last for hours attending teleconsultations. At that moment he stops resting from his long day of work, he stops sharing with his family, he stops enjoying his wife and children. He, without being aware of what he is doing, sacrifices quality time for work time.

I am in favor of knowing how to differentiate each role we exercise every day and to set limits in each one of them. If you are a doctor, you have to be a doctor within your schedule, in your work space. If you are a writer, be a writer within your work schedule. Once you decide to go home, you have to leave work at work.

The excuse that it is important to take the call in an emergency, or that you have to get up at dawn writing an article to be published the next day is not valid.

To continue with the previous example, if you are a doctor and you are at home, it is because in the clinic or hospital there are other competent professionals who can attend to emergencies, unless one arises with a particular patient and, because of affinity, you decide to attend to him/her, a case that does not happen all the time.

If you are a writer and you have to get up at dawn writing an article to be published in the morning, it is because you have not been competent with your time. You waste productive hours that you can take advantage of just because you decided to dedicate time to other topics that could have been taken care of later.

I call that a bad routine. The payment made to each worker, regardless of the profession, is for complying with a specific work schedule. What happens thereafter is not remunerated.

I applaud those responsible and productive professionals who champion their free time no matter how important a job may be. If you are assertive with time, dedicated, proactive, responsible, if you focus on what you do, then there can't be something left pending for the next day. If so, then from the start of your workday you can attend to it.

Depending on your line of work you should try to fulfill your responsibilities in the shortest time possible to have the most time available for you to enjoy life, because what is life then? Life, as the poet Jorge Luis Borges said "in case you don't know, is made only of moments, don't miss the now".

Of course, you have to enjoy life in the best possible way. In my case, I enjoy it without drinking liquor, without smoking, without taking drugs. Many people call me boring, but I, with the biggest smile on my face, reply that I don't need any stimulant to feel happy.

If I have two beers or two shots of *whiskey*, I fall asleep. Liquor makes me terribly sleepy. I think that, because I am such a relaxed man in life, the stimulating effect of liquor only makes me drowsy. I am not like other people who need a very high degree of drunkenness to feel happy.

I define happiness as an internal process that starts from

the emotional. The world of fame and show business re-
volves around concerts, rumbas, cocktails and presentations, but I do not enjoy them. Occasionally I have had to
attend a few due to work. However, if I am given a complimentary ticket, I give it to someone who will enjoy it, on the
condition that they tell me afterwards in detail everything
that happens.

Many times this strategy has given me the press release
before any other reporter. Those who have gone to these
shows for me have had to give me a lot of information,
such as the setlist of the artist who performed, what song
he/she performed, if anything unusual or extraordinary
happened, in short, they have provided me with all the information necessary to write a good press article without
the need to be present.

In short, I am one of the few press professionals who does
not enjoy parties, concerts or night events where I have
to wake up drinking liquor and dancing as if the world is
going to end to get a good article to publish.

There are those who have told me that these moments are
ideal to take advantage and do public relations. I believe
that the night offers nothing good and at night "all cats are
brown". I have gotten where I have gotten without having
to go to parties and without staying awake between music,
cigarettes and drinks. I don't see it as a waste of time, as
many will believe, because for some colleagues they are
very profitable moments, but for me it is not so productive,
you can get all the information without being present at
those meetings.

THE FINAL RESULT

Continuing with the previous point, for me it has not been
as necessary, as for other journalists, to be present at every gala show presented by the artists and to be intoxicat-
ed by them.

In some moments I had to cover the Ronda Award or the Meridiano de Oro Award, but when I had the necessary information for my publication, I would do the *Willie Mays*[1] , speaking in Creole, and I would go home early, just like in the Miss Venezuela events.

With propriety I can say then that very early in the morning, without being present at those events, I had a perfectly written note that, regardless of the process or the way in which I obtained the information, did not alter the result of writing the best possible, the most outstanding of that event.

I am a pragmatic man in my work. I know which are the key points that give me an impeccable press release. For example, in the Miss Venezuela pageants I did not consider it necessary to show up and stay four hours at the event to know what was going on, when I could watch it on television from the comfort of my home.

As an entertainment reporter, the important thing was to comply with the following information: who were the entertainers of the show, the singers who performed on stage, the musical themes that were interpreted, the performance of the contestants, which of them suffered a fall or misfortune on the catwalk, who gave the worst or the best answer to the *set of* questions, who was the winner and how was the honor roll.

As you can read, all this information could easily be obtained from someone who was present, from reading the minute-by-minute updates on the contest's website or from watching the television broadcast.

In my day-to-day life, I go to the important sources that have demonstrated seriousness in reporting. The *Billboard Music Awards,* for example, I did not watch them on televi-

1 Venezuelan expression meaning "to play the fool". Its origin comes from a baseball game of the 1955 Caribbean Series, when in a game between Navegantes del Magallanes and Cangrejeros de Santurce, Willie Mays had hit a spectacular home run, after twelve at-bats without a hit.

sion, nor was I present. In the morning, very early, I went to the media responsible for the broadcast such as *Univision, People en Español, Los Angeles Time*, news agencies, among others, and I covered my press release and delivered it to the media where I publish. I am practical, I value every minute of my day and I look for the information I need without much ado, that is my motto.

Despite being careful and conscientious in my work, my dynamic as an editor has not ceased to be annoying for some. However, I have never had any problems with my work, except for my "four dismissals" from the Dearmas Block, which, by the way, did not last more than an hour.

THE REVIEW THAT KILLED THE DISMISSAL

My first dismissal was for leaving the facilities and not closing the editing process of the magazines. I was four pages short in a magazine before it could go to press. At that time, I had a trip scheduled to Argentina, with a flight leaving at five in the morning.

As with any flight, I had to be at least a couple of hours beforehand at the airport, so I was unable to complete my work assignment, and because of the trip, I did not go to work. After noon, no one in the Dearmas Block knew about me and, of course, no one knew what material would complete the four pages.

When I arrived at the hotel, I checked my phone in my room and found a message with the termination notice. I read a message that told me not to even dare to explain anything, because I was already out on my ass.

I read it and replied that it was fine, perfect and that I understood it, but that in ten minutes they would receive all the necessary information to complete the information on the missing pages.

I sent them a very complete review of the hotel where I was staying, supported by photographs of its impeccable facilities, a gastronomic review of its restaurant, its magnificent dishes, photographs of its beautiful culinary presentations, a recipe from the chef and, as if to put the icing on the cake, its Michelin star, the highest gastronomic award for quality and excellence that a chef and a restaurant can receive.

I had done all that in the *Business Room* of the hotel, after my delicious meal. With that publication, the magazine looked great and was super benefited, so the final result killed the layoff.

The rest of my dismissals at the Dearmas Block were, likewise, for my disappearances in action. Those who worked at the Dearmas Block during my seventeen years as executive producer will know that, in the afternoons, the much appreciated and remembered director Gloria Fuentes would shout: "Where is Carlos Camargo?", "Look for Carlos Camargo!

Everyone was looking for me everywhere because something was missing for the magazines, because they needed to make the closing, because the fashion article was missing, among others. At that time, I was walking along the boulevard of Sabana Grande, or in the Ciudad Tamanaco Shopping Center, or I had gone home, or I was simply visiting my friends. In short, I was enjoying my life and everyone at the publishing house was crazy about my absences.

I knew what I had to do, because if there's one thing I have, it's responsibility and a sense of dedication to my work. The next day, at seven in the morning, I had the pictures, the fashion done, everything ready and I delivered it to the address. She just said *"Wow!"*.

I would give her interviews with Chiquinquirá Delgado, pictures of great showbiz photographers like Daniel Alonso or

Billy Cass, and she was surprised, because what I gave her was always of high quality.

That was how I justified my escapes and got my job back. The next day, my colleagues would ask me if they had made a mess of me, and I would just tell them no; what happened in the morning, they would ask me, and with a big smile I would answer "nothing, my boss invited me to have breakfast with her, because I had brought food for two".

MY OWN WAY

Many may think that my life is *hippie,* that I can be irresponsible and that I don't have a head for serious matters. Believe me, this is not so. My trick is to know how to manage my responsibilities.

You know I am not bound by time, however, my responsibilities are fulfilled and delivered on time.

I get up very early, write my notes, hand them in and immediately fulfill my other commitments.

Responsibility must never be lost, because if it is, the negative mark is indelible for those of us who work in this medium. I have not looked bad to anyone; I send the news, even if I am in the Conchinchina[2] .

IF I CAN DO IT, YOU CAN DO IT TOO

I have already told you a great part of my experiences, my tricks and my philosophy of life. My friend reader, I don't want you to read me just to know how I have managed to achieve the quality of life I enjoy today, I really want you to

---

2 Popular expression almost in disuse to refer to a very distant or remote place. Conchinchina was an ancient geographical and historical region that covered the southern third of present-day Vietnam.

learn to value the time you invest in your work and in your life, I want you to make an effort because the trick is in the focus, in the vision, in looking for change, because change is always good. If I could do it, you can do it too.

Don't think that I have always lived this way. Even if you have read before that I went in the afternoons to walk around the shopping malls or the boulevards of the city, it does not mean that I am unfulfilled, on the contrary, I have always been a diligent man, but, apart from that, I am a visionary.

During my absences from the office, I would go and plan an interview with actresses or artists such as Chiquinquirá Delgado, Athina Klioumi, Aguasanta Erminy, Johana Benedek, Deisy Arvelo or Scarlet Ortiz, for example. I would plan with them a photo shoot with professionals of the lens and diaphragm, and without scheduling or without being on schedule for any edition, I would deliver an article for my magazines. It was something amazing, because, without planning a prompt publication, the material arrived at the right time and needed for the magazine.

If you are a professional who loves what you do, follow your instincts and be a visionary. Being ahead of the curve and being proactive has its rewards. But yes, work is not the main thing, it is only a tool to live to the fullest.

I am not a man of methods as I have said before, I rather lean towards empiricism, trial and error, but there is something I always keep in mind: trust in my potential, intuition and risk, which has made me an agent of change.

I have always been very clear about the cardinal points that allow me to write a good press article and for those who are starting in this profession, I advise them to keep in mind the following *tips:* If the article reviews an event, for example, do not forget the place and date, the name of the event, name of the performer, content, extra references such as an invitation to another artist at the last minute or the appearance on stage of someone from the audience, the end and the behavior of the audience.

With this information you can put together a note of excellence. Be very descriptive so that the reader feels part of those present while reading. Do not lose details without being too wordy, that is, learn to be brief, concise and precise.

I dare to do things, to change styles, to innovate because I know I can do it, I trust in my talents, in my knowledge and in my strengths. I do not venture to do something without having at least the minimum notion to take on challenges.

We all suffer from the same fear of change, but we also have the strength to assume it. Just be confident and walk forward, confident, because you will always succeed, it is part of knowing how to live.

The blessing and the most beautiful gift a human being can have is to be able to wake up every day and do what you want. I work to be happy, I do not work to accumulate material goods and fill myself with ornaments, because life, as I see it, is like a Christmas tree.

The tree, with ornaments or not, will always be a tree. Life, with or without riches, will always be life and we all have to live it. Even if you fill your tree with lights, garlands and multicolored ribbons, it will always be a tree that sooner or later will be stripped of that clothing.

The essence of life is in the nakedness of that tree. Life is the same for everyone, so the task is to live with total surrender. We don't have to spend our existence filling our Christmas tree with ornaments, because if you pay attention, the ornaments are just extra things for others to see and marvel at what hangs on it.

The poor little tree will just be there, bearing the weight of the ornaments, begging for a chance to get rid of all that and go back to being a tree, pure and wild, wanting to show its essence and be happy.

I am not a crazy person who lives life *hippie* style, rather I consider myself an adventurer who lives life *happy,* while remaining normal, familiar with the environment, that is the difference, aware of my commitments and responsibilities, because if I fulfill them, I will enjoy each day more, that is my goal.

As a piece of advice, I will leave you with a very popular phrase:

"Do good, without regard to whom."

Ricardo Palma

(Homonymous story)

Peruvian Traditions (1872).

Shrouded in silence and anonymity

has raised cries of freedom.

Five hundred years have passed since his birth

And he's still as jovial as if he were twenty.

Incense cedar shirts have,

one or two pine, spruce and cypress.

His black heart has traced the poems

most beautiful of mankind.

The nobleman Don Quixote, Hamlet and

the Count of Monte Cristo,

are some of its immortal children.

He has recorded the life of Les Miserables,

the chronicle of a death foretold,

the tragic tale of a hen with her throat slit

and Macondo's One Hundred Years of Solitude,

since Ursula and José Arcadio ran away

of the Sierra to avoid a pig tail in their offspring.

America, from Alaska to Patagonia

thanks you for perpetuating the Constitution of your nations.

And it was the pencil that was the first to inspire

to boys and girls in the schools

to draw hearts on their notebooks,

as he has also been the last hero in

to tell the epic epics and epic battles

in the annals of history.

The pencil

A. Solak

CHAPTER 4

FROM THE PASTERN TO EDITION 2.0

The written word has always been my passion and my vocation. The early complicity between the graphite pencil, the quality of its strokes and an immaculate white sheet of paper helped me to perfect myself in the art of writing.

It is incredible to accept that the strength of an immense cedar can end up becoming the shirt that covers a mineral such as graphite and be for almost five centuries the preferred instrument of poets, writers, architects, draftsmen, designers, judges and executioners.

The modern world first emerged among its traces, before it became material. No technology, no matter how modern, can surpass it. It is known that every second five hundred pencils are manufactured.

Perhaps that is why global warming began, but already in the Amazon the so-called "pencil forests" or "sustainable forests" have begun to grow, to lessen the impact of the accelerated deforestation that is taking place in the rainforest.

With the pencil I wrote poems and met love. Yes, I fell blindly and madly in love with a beautiful German woman and as if to honor Aquiles Nazoa's sainete, I took "a leap backwards" with a beautiful German woman as black as night.

They will say there are no black German women, but mine was. And it was a torrid and productive romance. Long sleepless nights were spent in my room. She, submissive and quiet, but markedly rhythmic, let herself be carried away by the rapid pulsations I gave her between my hands.

She, a mischievous accomplice, let me tell her my stories with other women. She knew about my encounters with Chiquinquirá Delgado, Aguasanta Erminy, Sara Montiel, and even Celia Cruz, believe it or not.

She was a black Continental, the best typewriter I could have had and the one I became an expert typist with, the fastest in front of anyone. What did they think? I always talked about her, just in case. I'm sorry if they understood something else.

THE PASTILLE, THE MASTER FORMAT THAT MADE ME AN EXPERT WRITER

My beginnings as a newspaper editor were with the use of the so-called "cuartillas", letter-size sheets of paper with the Dearmas Block logo and twenty-five lines marked on their letterhead. The form also had its established boxes to place the name of the article and the magazine it belonged to.

I remember very well that we were instructed to write articles of two or three pages. I had to cover the entire form and I knew then that two or three pages of "such-and-such" articles meant not leaving any blank lines.

So it was every morning, my pleasant encounter with my typewriter, my ream of pages and the press releases to be transcribed.

A few years passed and the system underwent a great change: the transition from an analog method of writing on a printed form to the digital modernity that was opening up with the use of the first computers in publishing, some Jurassic IBM models with the DOS operating system, nothing graphic, only characters and a text editor that barely surpassed the typewriter.

It was *NewEdit*, the first editing program that I used, the truth is that it was nothing like our current text editors, so graphic and full of tools that make everything easier.

The transition from typewriter to computer was uncomfortable and difficult for many, to achieve it, we had to see classes in various workshops and courses led by a systems engineer named Luddy de los Reyes, who still works in the Dearmas Block.

With the demand for work, the nascent dial-up Internet, popularly known as *dialup*, we took another great evolutionary leap: the first computers of the little bitten apple arrived. I remember well that they were iMac G3 computers, they were "all in one". The same monitor, with a green casing, had all the equipment integrated. They were not like the archaic IBMs, with the big monitor and the *case* that served as a support.

These computers represented modernity, the step forward in technology, the latest technology at our fingertips. It was not so difficult to accept the change. The practice with the previous computers made us almost experts in the use of any computer.

Apple computers were much more versatile, faster and with the power to run design and editing programs. Of course the Internet and the use of email made things much easier.

The digital era we live in today is undoubtedly redesigning the face of the planet. Every year there are very marked changes and we have to adapt at incredible rates, really very accelerated.

Nowadays I no longer write in the old formats of pages that were printed and ready to be rolled up in the typewriter. I no longer need those monster computers to edit my publications. Just having a good *smartphone* that meets my needs, such as a good Internet connection and an available electricity point to recharge my cell phone battery is more than enough.

It's amazing how everything has changed in just a couple of decades. I no longer need a desk, a filing cabinet and a box of papers to review, read and sort to create my publications. Now I work anywhere in the world, from my phone, if I meet the needs specified above.

ETHICS AND PLAGIARISM IN THE AGE OF 2.0

Nowadays, finding information for a press release is just a click away. In the past, most of the time, print media reporters had to be on the scene to inform the population about what had happened or, failing that, we had to have someone very close to us to provide the information. The audacity of copying a press release as your own was almost unthinkable, because the sources of information were few, compared to today.

Many of my colleagues have had the misfortune -as they say- of being plagiarized by others for the publication of an article in a digital media. I say "as they say" because I have another perspective to face that fact, although I have not known that they have plagiarized my information, I would feel honored, I would take it as that my publication is so good that it served someone else.

Of course, if that person dares to give himself the authorship credits, it will be only in his mind, because for obvious reasons, such as my years in the medium and my marked editing style, would leave it uncovered.

I receive a lot of information because of my dedication to this profession in almost four decades of work, which has allowed me to amass a large number of contacts from other media that facilitate my work for my publications, in addition, I meet many interesting people, worthy of being interviewed and published in the press columns for the media I edit, that has given me prestige, because my notes are very particular, almost unique, they would hardly be taken as my own.

As an example of this I will tell you about Trino Jimenez, a musician and composer, musical director who worked in the National Orchestra System in Venezuela and who came to live in Nashville, Tennessee.

In a meeting I had with him, because he is my friend, he told me about a contract he had won with the University of Pretoria, in South Africa, to adapt some folk songs of the African country with jazz arrangements and symphony orchestra.

That press release was not born out of information that was on the news, as we say popularly, nor was it found on the Internet, it arose from the simplicity of a meeting of friends. I only asked him for more information, such as the lyrics of some songs, the meeting with Karendra Devroop, a very renowned musician in that nation, who is also the director of the university, the emergence of the project and the teamwork with him to carry out such a majestic mission.

My surprise was that after publishing my column *Camar-gonotas* in the newspaper 2001, also in *El Venezolano and Noti-America,* they sent the *links to* the director of the university, who was pleased and surprised, because the execution of the project was only for the university, with no desire to make it public, but was very pleased because, by way of thanks, he sent me through Trino Jimenez a CD of this production.

As you will see, reader friend, I get all my notes from the same original source, I am the first to give the news of the work of many of the artists because I am their PR, and without having to resort to searching on the Internet, I am, many times, the one who sets the tone and who gives the first *shot in* this profession.

ETHICS, THE BEST REFERENCE AND SOURCE OF RESPECT

Respect is not a value acquired by itself, it goes hand in hand with many other values. Ethics, honesty, education, humility and responsibility are its companions.

Getting to where I have come is due, to a great extent, to all those values that I bring with me, learned at home and over the years. However, my respect for others has made me worthy of the same value.

In my beginnings as a content writer for Bloque Dearmas, I did not know anyone. Although I had already worked in radio, I did not enjoy any kind of fame or renown, I came to them blank, with no contacts, no influence, no friends, no acquaintances. It was just me, my black German and my talent for writing.

My work as a columnist for the Bloque's magazines began to make me known among the journalists of the publishing complex, until Luis Moratinos and Rafael Fuentes Jr., deputy director of Bloque Dearmas, brother of my boss, director Gloria Fuentes, offered me the opportunity to be a record promoter. They already knew of my love of music and that I had experience in radio, besides having the ability to empathize with people.

I have always had that magic of connecting with people, my facility to engage in conversations and make friendships has made it very easy for me to meet very good people, regardless of their position or social status.

I treat everyone equally, with the same value, they are human beings like me and deserve all the consideration and respect possible. Have you ever heard from your parents and grandparents the phrase *"respect to be respected"*? Well, that is my motto and I live by it to the fullest.

As a promoter I was very successful, I managed to get the *singles* of the albums I took to the different radio stations to be played on the radio. I worked as a promoter for Manoca Récords, with producer Nico Acosta for Fama Récords and then for Pepe Récords. Stations like Tropical or Caracas 750, for other promoters were very difficult to convince. On the other hand, when I visited them and promoted the material, they immediately accepted it and played it. The radio man, Enrique Hoffman, and Jofre Majestracci Jr. were very supportive. In short, I had a sweet convincing power.

It is from that moment that I began to get involved with people in the music world, I began to have the support of the radio, which led me to have more contact with the written press. The people of Bloque Dearmas began to send me to press conferences, so I met great journalists of the moment, such as Carmela Longo, Elba Guillén, Maritza Martín, Iván Martínez Urbina, Iris Castro, Belén Chaparro, Marlene Castillo, Aquilino José Mata, Atamaica Nazoa, among others.

They were my references that I read in the show business articles of the different media. That's how they also began to know me, first as Carlitos Camargo, "the new" of *Ronda* or *Venezuela Farándula,* I rubbed shoulders with them and that generated a lot of excitement for me.

Once, at a press conference, I think it was during a visit of Luis Miguel to Caracas between 1986 and 1987 approximately, I met William Guzmán, a journalist who worked in Caracas as a correspondent of the Aragua state newspaper *El Siglo.* We talked a little about some artists, the work of the entertainment reporter and the profession in general. At the end of the press conference he gave me his card. As I liked him very much, I went to his office, in a shopping mall located in Chacaíto, east of Caracas. When he saw me, he received me with great affection.

We started talking pleasantly and out of nowhere, he started saying very nice things about me. He began to give me a series of advice that I treasure to this day. He has been one of the professionals, along with Rosana Ordoñez, Rafael Fuentes Jr., Gloria Fuentes, Apolinar Martínez, José Campos Suárez, Mirtha Figueroa, Roland Carreño, Virgilio Fernández, among others, who reached out to me and became my mentors to excel in my functions as I have always wanted to do.

Another thing that has given me my good reputation and respect from people in the show business is that I have never lent myself to write a press release unfounded in gossip or with the intention of causing discredit.

I began to set my own editorial line, one that gave no place to rumors or hallway gossip. Even if it had veracity, I was opposed to writing any unhealthy commentary on the artists; I consider it an ugly strategy to sell news.

My style is based on highlighting the best of each artist, newcomer in the media or famous, I take their positive and human side, the good performance of his career, the projects in execution and those to come, it is the right and ethical, what they taught me, of them I only take the news, not the showbiz notes, that's for others to take care of.

Now, my advice to those who read me, whether they are social communicators or not, is that you should always work ethically, mark your own path without taking advantage of your colleagues or imitating others. If you are going to extract information from someone else, do not publish it as your own, give credit to the one who really developed it.

There is nothing nicer than receiving recognition for an authentic work, that is recognized as your own, that has your own style, so, if you do not have a defined style, start marking it, always based on respect. Be innovative, friendly and treat everyone equally, because in your workplace everyone is valuable, from the lady or man who throws away the garbage and cleans the desk, to the artist who makes the news, the media director who publishes your report or the colleague next to you, who complements you with his or her idea.

You have to know and be recognized by the people in your work environment, if you are anonymous you don't grow. Plants grow slowly in the shade, but if they are in the light, they grow stronger and faster. Support your new colleagues, keep the chain, you did not get to where you have arrived alone, there was always someone who approached you and gave you their tricks and suggestions. It's your turn to do the same and always be grateful.

Work with love, give the best of you, always keep in mind that you must be someone who adds to the team, not subtract, remember that there are natural laws that are fulfilled, such as sowing and harvesting, you will only reap what you have sown, the quality of your seed depends on your treatment of others, then do not complain.

THE RISE OF FAKE NEWS

Social networks, apart from being instant information channels, have become fertile ground for the proliferation of *fake news*. They start as a simple rumor and end up so big, that sometimes they are scary. Nowadays, anyone who has an account on a social network and reaches a certain number of followers, believes he has the right to call himself a social communicator.

My advice to those "social communicators" graduated in social networks is not to become repeater antennas if they have not confirmed the source before. Being a social communicator is not the one who first publishes a press release, but the one who assumes responsibility for the impact that its publication may cause, being a social communicator is the one who verifies in several responsible sources if the news he is going to publish is true or not, if it is going to help others or not, if it is going to inform for the good of others or not.

Publishing information means understanding that everything you disclose about that person will positively or negatively affect his or her career and will impact his or her prestige in the same way. If you are not going to be a repeater for the positive, then it is better not to say anything. If the artist or person doesn't deserve a positive note because they are simply a jerk, then it's best to say nothing, there are plenty of unethical people who will take care of that.

THE ESSENCE IS THE ITSELF

In my almost four decades of work as an entertainment reporter, I have had to keep pace with technological changes, but that has not affected my essence as a professional. Many have come to me to grow as artists by the hand of my promotion, as there are also those who have approached me with the intention of taking advantage of my wide projection in the media to take advantage and publish a press release that harms their competition.

I have never had the need to do anything like that, I have never lent myself to be a repeater of gossip and I am convinced that I will not do so in the future. I keep my integrity and I have the utmost respect for the integrity of others.

I am a promoter of good things, because those are the things that should prevail in the media. Unfortunately, there are many people who continue to work to damage the image of artists. I think that does not deserve dedication, whoever works badly, immediately writes his fame, the public is wise and always knows how to give the deserved treatment to their artists. Those who are maintained is because they have earned it, those who do not, already know the answer.

At this an expert in the law appeared and, to test Jesus, asked him this question: "Master, what must I do to inherit eternal life?"

Jesus replied: "What is written in the law? How do you interpret it?"

In reply the man quoted: "Love the Lord your God with all your heart, with all your being, with all your strength and with all your mind," and: "Love your neighbor as yourself."

Jesus said to him, "Well answered. Do this and you will live."

But he wanted to justify himself, so he asked Jesus: "And who is my neighbor?"

Jesus answered: "A man was going down from Jerusalem to Jericho, and fell into the hands of robbers. They stripped him of his clothes, beat him and went away, leaving him half dead. A priest happened to be on the same road, and when he saw him, he turned aside and went on his way. So also a Levite came to that place and, when he saw it, he turned away and continued on his way.

But a Samaritan who was on a journey came to the man and, seeing him, had compassion on him. He came near, dressed his wounds with wine and oil, and bandaged them. Then he mounted him on his own mount, took him to a lodge and took care of him. The next day, he took out two silver coins and gave them to the owner of the lodging.

Take care of it for me," the Samaritan said, "and whatever you overspend, I'll pay you back when I get back."

Jesus asked: "Which of these three do you think demonstrated being the neighbor of the one who fell into the hands of thieves?"

"He who had compassion on him," replied the expert in the law.

"Go and do the same," Jesus concluded.

Parable of the Good Samaritan

Luke 10:25-37 (NIV)

CHAPTER 5

THE IMPORTANCE OF PUBLIC RELATIONS

I n my childhood and already a bit in my early teenage years I loved reading the Bible and writing those great stories, like the parables of Jesus and the beautiful stories of Genesis. The Bible has always been an enchanting book, full of wisdom within everyone's reach.

You don't have to be a religious person to understand it or to look for answers to our questions when introspecting.

If you read it carefully, you will not only find the philosophy of life of the good Christian, you will also find beautiful stories that fit in with universal history, you will find poetry and you will also find ideal advice to achieve success in all aspects.

If you pay more attention, the Bible will give you the master key to live in perfect harmony with everyone and every other species in this world, one that belongs to all of us equally. Among these tips we find one that has to do with respect for others.

The human species is the one that currently dominates the world and marks supremacy over the other species, but how did it achieve such a feat if physically we are at a disadvantage before other species that surpass us in strength and speed?

Apart from having greater intelligence, we understood that "together, side by side, we are much more than two", as described by the Uruguayan poet Mario Benedetti. We understood that our success is anchored to the success of the other, if I help him, I help me, if you help me, you help yourself, it's as simple as that. Isn't this called public relations?

PUBLIC RELATIONS, A WAY OF LIFE

There is a career in Public Relations, but its success comes more from the heart, more from the soul, more from social interaction, more from dealing politely with people and understanding what is needed and what is wanted, more than understanding theories that talk about the importance of helping each other to achieve success.

I am a journalist who fulfills a dual role: being a reporter for different media outlets and being an event promoter for various artists. As a news editor I have received a countless number of representatives of artists, record labels or event organizers with information to be published in my columns.

I have received them and I have told them what is really newsworthy. Some promoters focus on highlighting the business work rather than the artist, which for me is not news and I have made it known, the artist will always be the protagonist of the information.

Many of these representatives have treated some of my colleagues as if they were one of their employees, as if the reporter has to thank them for the news they bring them, and moreover, they go overboard, which reflects an arrogance that is accompanied by demands and conditions for the press release to be published without giving anything in return.

Not that you have to do it, but you have to understand that the relationship between reporter and agent has to be carried out as a symbiosis, that is to say, that both sides benefit equally. While the reporter reflects what can be a positive and admirable image of the artist, something very valuable for his rise to fame, the artist and his representatives have to treat the social communicator with equal respect and admiration.

In my work as an event promoter in Venezuela for companies such as Emporio Group, who brought to the country major international projects such as

J. Balvin, Violetta, Melendi, Romeo Santos, and more, or my work with Only Tickets Eventos in the animatronic presentations of "Dinosaurs, a Jurassic Experience", or "The Ice Age" and my work with Peluche Productions, the organizers of major salsa events like Las Noches en Nueva York or other events like Amanecer Gaitero at the Poliedro in Caracas, I always understood and treated the writer well so that he/she would write the best press release.

He provided them with as much information as possible, gave each reporter covering the event their two complimentary tickets to ensure their attendance and guaranteed them full attention during the concert.

Colleagues said: "I like the concerts that Carlos promotes because he is always looking out for the editor".

In the shows organized on the terrace of the Centro Comercial Ciudad Tamanaco (CCCT), with Luis Moratinos, when we would bring Gilberto Santa Rosa with several pipers, I would ask the organizers to give me my thirty complimentary tickets and VIP passes to hand them out to the journalists and guarantee as many reviews as possible in the media.

Many times the businessmen argued with me, but I insisted, so they ended up giving in and pleasing me. They just had to give the tickets and as much attention as possible, they understood that without the press there was no success for the event.

At first they did not understand the strategy, until they finally understood that with a better treatment towards the press they would receive from them great articles about the artist and about the event in general in the different media, which added credibility, trust and respect for the businessmen, so they could offer their services to other artists who wanted to organize events with them, it was the best publicity they could have.

I lived those experiences as a media editor, and since I already knew the dynamics, I put myself in the shoes of the professional who attended my promotions. I attended many events where I did not receive complimentary tickets, but they demanded a good press release. That's why I educated the organizers and representatives of the artists, if they worked with me they had to accept my clauses, otherwise, they didn't count on me.

There is a good anecdote about a Romeo Santos concert that I promoted in Venezuela. After he split from the group Aventura, he launched his solo career and toured internationally, even singing at the Poliedro in Caracas in 2014.

For two years I was in charge of being his promoter in Venezuela. At his concert I arranged for me about fifty chairs that were intended for guests of the media. At first they were uncomfortable with the number of courtesy guests, but I stood firm in my request, because I knew that the strategy aimed to cause a positive impact on the gala in question.

Once the press representatives were in place, a few minutes before the start of the concert, Romeo's *road manager* asked me to help him bring a girl on stage. There was a promotional song for the tour that contained a scene in which Romeo was seducing a woman. He asked me for a model, and I immediately told him that I had the ideal person.

Among the press representatives there was a girl named Eulymar Vargas, a reporter for *Noticias 24,* a nice chubby girl who was always very affectionate with me. I called her to be the model to go on stage without revealing anything to her. She had no idea what I was up to.

The concert had already started and this girl was a devoted *fan* of the artist. At first she was kind of restless because she wanted to stay in her seat and enjoy the whole event. But I was emphatic in asking for her collaboration. I told her that I had no one else to count on, that I was alone and that she was the only one who could help me.

She, a bit nervous, accepted and accompanied me backstage. The road manager was there, and I told him that she was the girl who was going to collaborate with us.

He said: "Perfect, are you sure?"

"Of course, she is the ideal one."

Immediately, a young man from production arrived, took her by the hand and led her to the stage. She was very nervous and just asked: "Carlos, what do I do?"

"Nothing, don't worry, they will guide you."

Upon arriving on stage, she was greeted by Romeo Santos and invited to sit in a chair on the stage. This woman almost had a heart attack from the emotion of being chosen for this purpose.

Romeo Santos immediately began his show. He approached her, and the first thing he asked her was her name, he also asked her if she was alone or accompanied by her boyfriend or husband. The girl told him that she was alone, that she had attended unaccompanied.

He started with his song, took one of her hands and ran it in a caressing motion down her body. Then he stopped and asked her what kind of kiss she liked. She, like every girl, told him the romantic kiss. Romeo then asked her if she knew the impromptu or surprise kiss. She said no and at that instant the artist kissed her quickly on the mouth.

The whole audience went wild. The hullabaloo was impressive and the scene became the biggest showbiz news reported in all the media. Eulymar Vargas thanked me effusively for taking her into account for such a memorable scene. *Ronda* magazine made a great review of the moment and the image of the young journalist was among its pages.

It was the best decision I made when I chose her. She was not the girl with model attributes, she was a normal girl, with some extra pounds, like most women, who also falls in love, who likes kisses and who also has the right to be seduced by an attractive young man.

Apart from the value I place on women, the other important note is that you have to keep your essence. I am not a man who suffers from professional misgivings. Even though the reporter did not work in any of the media I work for, for me that was not the important thing. In this profession what really matters is that we can all count on each other, regardless of whether or not we are colleagues in the same media.

The work of the social communicator is to bring the news to the public, so that each person can read it, listen to it or watch it and enjoy the content, this will guarantee the continuity of our profession, it will make it continue, otherwise if we are not read, if we are not seen and if we are not heard, then our work will disappear.

The success of my continuity in the media for almost forty years is not exclusively due to my talent, the real success is in the invaluable support given to me by my colleagues in the different media. An example of this is the support they have given to my column *Camargonotas*, which was born in the magazine *Venezuela Farándula*, was also read in the magazine *Variedades,* and later in *Diario 2001* and today is also published in other media such as *El Venezolano* de Miami, *El venezolano* de Madrid, *NotiexpressColor,* among others.

Now, in the middle of the 2021 semester, *it has* begun to be published in affiliates of FOX, NBC, CBS, Miami *Herald Newspaper, Times,* and more than fifty prestigious digital media throughout the United States and in English.

This achievement is not made by any journalist, or any editor or any person, it is achieved by a professional who does not see his counterpart as competition, but sees him as his equal and with whom he can collaborate to also receive the same treatment. It is the result of good public relations management.

RESPECT, THE GREATEST POWER FOR EFFECTIVE PUBLIC RELATIONS

The power of public relations is based on the equal respect that you can give to all the people around you without belittling their work, from the lady or man who cleans the office, to the director of the newspaper, magazine cr television channel where you work, with good treatment you get respect and admiration in every profession.

Another thing to take into consideration is to facilitate the work of each one of them. Colleagues have come to me asking for little things, such as a vertical photograph of a particular artist, or the telephone number of one of their representatives, or even the possibility of an interview with one of them, and I have kindly given it to them, and if I don't have it, I look for it and give it to them.

I like to serve them and be useful to them because they have been the same with me. My career, as I said before, has been consolidated by my good treatment with people and the good treatment they have given me. Natural law of sowing and harvesting.

We cannot believe we are self-sufficient or all-powerful to do things, we always have to turn to someone, either because they know more, because they know the one who knows, because they made you feel good in your moment of affliction and doubts, or because they simply gave you the coffee you needed to stay awake in your work.

Public relations is based precisely on relating empathetically with everyone. Unfortunately, people become friends with positions and not with people, without understanding that people will always be above positions.

Another good piece of advice I can give you, my friend reader, is to keep in mind that the world is like an acetate record, it spins and spins, sometimes at thirty-three revolutions per minute, sometimes at forty-five revolutions per minute and you don't know in which groove you will have to take the leap and get out. Today you are here, tomorrow it may be your turn to leave or be somewhere else.

There are those who have come to feel vetoed because they are unable to publish anything in a particular media. When you look back at your dealings with the media director who is in charge, you will understand that in the past your dealings with him were not respectful or professional, and that is why you have come to feel affected in your functions.

This is the slogan that you must fulfill as a life task: you must give the right value to each person, as a person, regardless of the position he or she holds, because that person who today has a minor position, tomorrow may assume a managerial position and return the same treatment you gave him or her. Do not expect to harvest apples when you have sown hot peppers. Remember that there are family members who follow in your footsteps, and the treatment you give to others may affect the path they are just beginning to walk.

To summarize, the pillars of any profession are based on respect, good communication and good treatment of others. If you comply with this triad of values, you ensure 50% of success in your career.

FRIENDSHIPS VERSUS CONTACTS

Whoever does this job must have good friends and good contacts to facilitate the work. Contacts are all the people that appear in your personal phone book, from A to Z.

In my address book I have all kinds of contacts, from the

guy who prints the label on the acetate disc, or the newspaper salesman, to the most renowned model or artist of the moment.

In Caracas I had as my favorite contacts the owners of the different kiosks that sold newspapers and magazines, both regional, national and international. There were four kiosks of my preference. One was located in Chacaíto, at the exit of the subway station, where I got all the national and regional press, from *Panorama* in Zulia, to *El Sol de Margarita* in Nueva Esparta. The other one was at the exit of the subway station in Altamira, where I bought the magazines that arrived from abroad. The other two complementary kiosks were on the fourth avenue in Los Palos Grandes and another very large one in Colinas de Bello Monte.

I had a practice that worked for me for a long time. I made friends with the newsstand owners so that they would put aside for me all the newspapers and magazines that I regularly consulted. I didn't do it as a journalist, in that case I did it as press officer of the artists who hired me.

I had a lot of appreciation and sympathy for the owner of the kiosk in Chacaíto. He was a man well into his old age. As he was the one who had the most newspapers from the different correspondents in the country, he was the one from whom I bought the press.

I reached an agreement with him to pay him something extra if he would classify the newspapers that reviewed the artists I represented.

For him it wasn't work, because he was a kind of bookworm, but a newsstand version. He read everything he could get his hands on, so he took advantage and classified the newspapers that reviewed my clients, such as Oscar D'León, Olga Tañón, Emporio Group, Only Tickets Eventos, and others.

I carefully read the names of the reporters of the different news spaces of each newspaper, their contact e-mails and, if possible, their telephone numbers, and copied them in a notebook, thus creating my own agenda of regional correspondents.

Every day I would take one area of the country and call reporters from those states. I would introduce myself as the press officer of the different artists I represented. I would do it before each type of reporter of the different regional newspapers of the country. I would make myself known and ask for their collaboration in case I needed it from them and I would also put myself at their disposal, besides asking for their address to send them some discs as a gift.

I did it with the economic, social, entertainment and political reporters, although I never asked many of them for any collaboration.

Many were surprised to be called from Caracas for this purpose. They claimed that no journalist had ever called them to ask for their collaboration. They felt that they were taken into account and that they were treated as equals.

On several occasions he traveled with the artists on a national tour. With some cunning he would convince them to visit the different radio stations in each state and he would also take advantage of the opportunity to do some national tourism.

As I am devoted to Dr. José Gregorio Hernández, I took many of them to Isnotú, Trujillo state, the birthplace of the "doctor of the poor" and took the opportunity to go to his birthplace and pray for the care and strength of his talent. Things like that remain now as beautiful anecdotes for them and for me.

In this way I began to create a large list of contacts, many of them later became great friends of mine. I want to make an emphasis with this, not all of them are today my friends, many of them are just very good contacts not only in Venezuela, I have also amassed a large list of good contacts and good friends in Panama, Dominican Republic, Puerto Rico, Colombia, United States, France, Spain, Germany, Italy, Argentina, Chile, the truth in many countries.

They are not my friends or good contacts because I only call them when I need them, that is the mistake, the contact and the friend should also be called to say hello, to know about them, to remind them that they also count on you, that is reciprocity and good relations. I consider that it is in very bad taste to make the call out of interest. That is not what public relations is about, it is about giving the good treatment you wish to receive.

Now I will tell you about my friends. The ones I have I have harvested and I have earned them based on respect and good treatment as a professional and as a human being.

Don't think that because I have been working with artists for more than ten years I can treat them with abuse of confidence and go beyond the limits, on the contrary, the more confidence I have, the more respect I have. I have friends that I have gained through my work. Some of the artists I represent I consider friends and they consider me their friend.

I have clients who have invited me to their homes and have hosted me there, others have taken me on vacations. Porfi Baloa, for example, on one of my birthdays gave me a trip to Cancun and like him, others have given me trips to Santo Domingo, to Colombia, to name a few.

There is a very nice anecdote that happened with a trip I had to make to Santo Domingo to cover an event. I made a mistake with the ticket and bought one with another destination. When I realized it, I insistently asked the airline ticket agent to change my ticket, because I had mistakenly asked for a ticket to another city. I was lucky, because the young man did so, which he had no obligation to do, in any case, I had to assume my responsibility quietly.

Once my ticket was changed, the next day I boarded the

plane to Santo Domingo. I noticed that I did not have the address of the event and I had only a hundred dollars in my pocket. So after struggling to get my ticket changed, I was stuck in Santo Domingo not knowing where to go and unable to stay in a hotel because I did not have enough money to do so.

Therefore, I decided to return to Venezuela, but there was a detail: there was only one daily flight to the Dominican Republic from Venezuela and on the same plane I arrived, that same plane left at once for Venezuela.

Things were getting complicated and I couldn't figure out what to do. I remembered that once Chiquinquirá Delgado recorded a commercial in Venezuela for a Dominican banker. At that time, businessmen from other Latin American countries preferred to shoot their commercials in Venezuela because it was much cheaper than shooting in their own countries and of better quality, besides having the most beautiful models in the world.

Since we had a good relationship, I decided to call him and explain my situation. He immediately took care of me, listened to me and gave me all the help I needed to be at ease. He immediately sent a driver to pick me up at the airport and take me to a hotel to spend the weekend, with all lodging and food expenses paid.

Early Monday morning he sent the driver again to pick me up at the hotel and take me to the airport. It was a very kind action on his part, for which I will always be grateful.

If I had not been the way I am, to respect all my peers and treat them with affection and equality, something like this would never have happened to me. I have friendships in this environment of more than twenty or thirty years which I value very much and I am very grateful to all of them, because they have not only given me their love and respect, they have taught me, they have formed me as a great professional and that is invaluable.

MEETINGS AND REUNIONS WITH CONTACTS FROM MY SOCIAL NETWORKS

If anyone has harvested contacts by chance or by fortune of fate, it has been me. I have had such crazy encounters through social networks that can go from a Colombian guerrilla in the mountains of Valle del Cauca, in the Colombian-Venezuelan border, to an encounter with followers of my networks in the Canary Islands.

Back when the Blackberry phone was the king of mobile telephony, the famous Blackberry PIN was all the rage. People added countless contacts thanks to the ease with which it could be done. It was an alphanumeric hexadecimal code. They dictated a series of numbers and letters associated with the device and that was enough to belong to the large list of *BBM (Blackberry Messenger)* groups.

More than once it happened to me that while adding a contact, I misspelled one of the digits and a different contact was saved, or I made combinations with a friend's pin number and found an active user from another country or state that I had never seen before. However, I did not delete them, I kept them and started writing to them as if I really knew them. That's how I ended up in a guerrilla chat room in Colombia.

One of those contacts that I always greeted, without realizing it, added me to a group of young soldiers who patrolled the border jungle between Colombia and Venezuela. I don't know if it was to guard the coca crops or to destroy them. What was certain was that I spent hours chatting with those guys, until, as a joke, I added Pamela Toledo, coordinator of the digital newspaper *La Patilla.*

The first thing he asked me was if I was crazy and how I had gotten involved with those military men. We started chatting for hours, until one of them asked Pamela to be his girlfriend. Going with the flow, we said yes and I sent him pictures of her. This very excited boy sent an itinerary for the meeting: we had to get to Valle del Cauca, a jeep from the mayor's office would pick her up and take her to a sector in the middle of the jungle that would transport her through the mountains on a two-day trip until she reached her destination. It was really crazy.

Just as I had unlikely encounters in the middle of the jungle, I had encounters with real acquaintances. Once I posted on my Instagram account that I would travel to the Canary Islands with maestro Oscar D'León, who would show off his voice in a small presentation in the archipelago.

My surprise was that as soon as I arrived at the airport I was met by an old friend I had not seen for a long time. I asked him how he knew about me, because I had long since lost contact with him. He told me that thanks to Instagram he found out that I would be traveling to the Canary Islands and since he lived near the airport, he dared to receive me to surprise me and so it was. I introduced him to Maestro Oscar and his wife and we shared a very nice moment at the airport.

There is no greater gift than a friendship and nothing more effective to cultivate it than respect and good treatment. Do not neglect those you have in your address book, write to them from time to time, not out of interest, do it out of courtesy, respect and consideration. Remember that the world is a handkerchief and that it spins and spins like an acetate record, we do not know the turns that life takes and it is always better to have a friend and not need it, than to need it and not have it.

In tobacco, in coffee, in wine,

at the edge of the night they rise

like those voices that sing in the distance

without knowing what, along the way.

Lightly brothers of destiny,

dark, pale shadows, they frighten me

the flies of the habits, they support me

to stay afloat amidst so much whirlpool.

The dead talk more, but in the ear,

and the living are warm hand and roof,

sum of what has been gained and what has been lost.

So one day in the shadow boat,

of so much absence will shelter my chest

this ancient tenderness that names them.

Poem Friends

Julio Cortázar

A pilgrim on his route came across a village. At the entrance of the town was located the cemetery and, surprised, he approached curiously to look at the tombs. Great was his surprise to discover that all the tombs marked the exact ages of the deceased. "Martín Pérez: eight years, three months, six days, four hours." "Lucía Silva: seven years, eight months, nine days, one hour".

It appears that they all died in childhood. What had happened in this town to make people die so young?

Dismayed and distressed by his discovery, he approached the center of town with concern. There he noticed that the inhabitants were very old and curiously asked one of them: "What happened to the children? The cemetery is full of children's graves."

The old man, with a smile on his face replied: "Nothing has happened, no child has died in this town. What happens is that we have a very particular custom. When we turn fifteen, we receive a notebook as a gift to write down the duration of those moments that we consider to be our greatest experiences. From then on, every time we live something intense, we open the notebook and write in it. On the left side we write down what we enjoyed,

On the right, how long did that joy last: did he meet his girlfriend and fall in love with her? How long did that enormous passion and the pleasure of meeting her last? One week, two? Three and a half weeks? And then, the emotion of the first kiss, how long did it last, a minute and a half, two days, a week? And so we write down in the notebook every moment, every joy, every full and intense feeling. When someone of us dies, we open his notebook and add up the time he enjoyed in life. On his grave will not appear his chronological time of life, but his kairos time, the sum of the quality time he lived."

Brief account of the story *The Seeker*
Jorge Bucay

CHAPTER 6

THE TOOLS TO MAINTAIN SUCCESS

Western culture is anchored to a model of social life that was designed by the ancient Greeks. From them we learned philosophy, law, democracy and enriched our literature thanks to their mythological gods, one for each human emotion, passion, fear and longing.

Happiness is one of those human passions that is represented in his pantheon. Dionysus, the god of wine and madness, is its highest representative. But happiness is not based on drunkenness and madness; happiness, according to the definition of the Greek philosophers, is the state of plenitude that each person can reach; being happy is a responsibility that each person has with himself and is not in what surrounds him.

As happiness depends on each person, we must enjoy each day and be happy with what we have, without forgetting that the days are limited by Chronos, the Greek god of linear time, and that in order to maintain and not die, he gobbles up each of our days.

Happiness, then, from my perception, is anchored to time. And the fact is that time is not only that which runs chronologically from the beginning of our days to the end of them.

There is also Aion time, the time of life. Plato designates the intensity of the time of human life as a temporality that is neither successive nor numerable but intensive. Aion has been represented as a serpent that bites its own tail and that indicates the eternal return.

This time is cyclical, it represents the course of life: to be born, to grow, to die. Aion, as an eternal god, without beginning or end, is the teacher of all. He who makes a mistake and does not rectify it, will make it again and again, until he learns from it and makes things right.

But the most beautiful time of which we should be more aware of its existence and be educated to benefit from it, is Kairos time.

This time is not governed by Chronos, owner of quantitative chronological time, nor by Aion, always present time that sees the past and the future at the same time; this time is qualitative, fleeting and unexpected, Kairos time is fast and instantaneous.

Kairos is a capricious pixie son of Zeus and Tyche, goddess of fortune. He appears when least expected. We Christians call it "God's timing is perfect". My faith is my time. That is how I think and live. God is the only owner of time. He is not subject to our time, much less to how "rushed" or "unhurried" we are in doing things. He has His purposes, and His purposes are totally tied to His time, not ours. Time on earth is a blink of an eye from God's eternal perspective. A second is no different from an eon; a billion years pass as seconds to the eternal God.

Surely it has ever happened to you that you want to do something and you say "wow, I don't have time", and days or weeks later you think "why didn't I do it? Well, this happens to many people who sometimes are not aware that there are things that do not turn back, that the "would have" does not exist and that it is essential to value our here and now. To be clear about what we want in our life and at what moment will help us to take advantage of the time in the best way.

Therefore, here I tell you about three times that if you know how to manage them, they will be your best allies in your various projects in life:

1. **Time to heal.** Some people forget that there is a "time to heal". This applies from an accident, a love breakup, a loss of a loved one or a job.

2. **Formative or creative time.** Our character is forged from everything that happens to us in our existence. To acquire wisdom you

need practice and the development of skills and tests that you can only obtain with time.

3. **Time that does not return.** There are three things that do not return: words, time and opportunities. Words like "I would have done", "I would have told him", "we would have gone", in short, a series of afflictions that do not leave us in peace, this when we see that people, ages or places are no longer there and that we would do anything for them to return. That is life. Let's value time in the positive. And how do we do it? We just have to dedicate less chronological time to our lives and add more quality time. How do we do it? Get your work done in the shortest time possible and as a reward take advantage of that time to live, grow and enjoy, it will be your greatest gift.

WE MUST TAKE ADVANTAGE OF THE TIME

Making the most of your time does not mean getting up very early in the morning and working late into the night. Of course, "the early bird catches the light water", but the goal of catching light water is not always subject to getting up early.

This saying is addressed to inexperienced young people who need it for their learning. They are those who need to gain experience. The earlier they get up, the more time they have available to absorb as much knowledge, to gather clear water.

Those who have become experts do not have to get up early for clear water; they are the source of knowledge for the apprentices. Experience is the first resource to take into account when it comes to making the most of time.

In the beginning, when I was just a seventeen-year-old kid starting out in content writing, I kept to my schedule to the letter. I would arrive very early in the morning and leave at the end of the workday, but that was only at the beginning. My dealings with that clock that pigeonholes me, that forces me to punch a time clock, have been nil. In fact, I don't wear a watch and the ones I have are kept in storage. I have never bowed to it, I am indomitable to its ends.

As soon as I understood the dynamics of the job, I quickly pulled out my essay and went to each floor of the editorial block. I observed what was being done in each department, learning from each one of them.

Little by little I was acquiring other knowledge that complemented what I already knew, which allowed me to have a wider field of expertise in the publishing world. I no longer only wrote, I understood more about production in general.

Creativity is one of my strengths. As magazines from abroad came to the editorial office to read their information and take from them material for our publications, I realized that we had to change the dynamics. Using reports from other countries and publishing them in our magazines seemed to me an uncreative and tasteless task, I opted for the creation of my own material, to report what was happening in our country.

My time spent on my informal tours of the other departments helped me to understand the work of publishing. I was never satisfied with just writing, I had to understand the whole process, the advertising process. So, in addition to writing, I sold the magazine ads myself.

Also, as I had a preference to use photographs of Venezuelan models for my publications, I started to create my image bank. I saw the need we had for this resource. My escapes were no longer for the other departments, so I began to go abroad to create my images. I had the support of *Mariela's New Styles* modeling agency.

Likewise, I did not use the photographers of the publishing house, I hired private photographers as an exchange, I put their names in the magazines and provided them with the 35 mm photographic roll. They had a better eye and more availability to do the job. I used the best: Miguel Angel Alonso, Billy Cass, Daniel Alonso, Juan Carlos Rodriguez, Fidel Teran and Guillermo Felizola, among others.

The right investment of my time has led me to many achievements. I quickly grew as a professional in the Dearmas publishing block and quickly became known in the industry.

Do you think that simply being a good copywriter has gotten me this far down the road? Aside from my talent for writing, my hunger to know more, my daring style for innovation, or the value of commitment to doing things well, it's the fact of getting my work done in the shortest time possible to have more time for myself that has truly allowed me to go out and get what I needed to enjoy my work and stay in the medium. That is my success and my greatest triumph.

INTUITION DEVELOPS WITH EXPERIENCE

Experience comes with time. He is our great teacher and the one who builds our path. While he does so, we follow behind, attentive to what happens on our journey without ceasing to take notes of what we see. If we do not pay attention, how do we become experts? We get lost on other paths and stray from the goal.

Time provides you with an accumulation of tools, such as relationships with other professionals in the environment in which you work, contacts, knowledge, mastery and the sense of smell or sense to do the job well.

In my case, I was able to find the right tone for my press articles thanks to the sum of all these tools. There were many occasions when the news found me and not me it.

In my escapes from the office, when some colleagues thought I was running away and not fulfilling my duties, I stumbled upon the news. It was a gift from God, as if I was being called to be there at the right time.

When I went to the TV channels to visit my models who were also actresses or actors, to make a set of photographs, I observed how the artists who were inactive arrived at the channel, what did my intuition tell me, based on my experience, that artist did not go to visit, there is something else.

Once Jean Carlo Simancas went to Venevisión on an occasion when I was there, meeting with an actress. When I saw him, my alarm bells immediately went off: "What is he doing here if he was in Miami? He's not in any novela or other program, what's he doing here? I immediately called one of my friends at Venevisión and asked her if there was any new project in development.

When he answered me, he told me that yes, there was a new project and that they were looking for talent to renew the contract. Then, I asked him if Jean Carlo Simancas was in that group and he said yes, he was one of the artists that were called by the channel.

After that confirmation, I already had a press release. How did I acquire it? That journalistic sense of smell developed by experience is what helps me to tie up logical ends. To be a journalist you have to be daring, curious and fearless, if you are not, then this is not your career.

I do not cover the events section in the media, although I have done so on several occasions, thanks to the tutelage of José Campos Suárez, a renowned Venezuelan journalist who is successful in that field, but if I am driving and I see an accident, I stop, get out of the car and go to the place of the event and pass the story on to the colleague who does cover that news section.

Once there was a shooting in a town near my residence;

after the shooting stopped I went to the place to find out what had happened. I immediately called one of my friends at Telemundo Channel 51 and passed on the information, who was the first to broadcast it.

In order for a young journalist to be successful in this field, he/she must rub shoulders with the social environment, with the greatest number of people who work in the media, he/she must be an investigator, curious, observant, in this way he/she will develop instinct and acquire tools that will allow him/her to obtain the news at the least expected moment.

THE PROPER USE OF SOCIAL NETWORKS

Social networks have become the favorite tool of those of us who make news. They allow us to be everywhere without being there, a kind of omnipresence that shows us the development of the news story we want.

However, its use can become a double-edged sword if we do not know how to use it and we become a kind of repeater antennae of the famous *fake news.*

On one occasion, Oscar D'León's social media *manager* called me to tell me that Tania Sarabia had passed away. I immediately told him: "Look boy, who told you that? Don't publish something that is not verified. That is a lie."

"But how do you know? Everyone says so through the media."

"But who is everybody? You have to learn to look for information from reliable sources. Did you search Tania's networks? Did you contact a family member or close friend? Did any serious news media publish it?"

"No, but it's on Twitter."

A few minutes later, Tania Sarabia herself denied her

death.

You must learn to be responsible and ethical when publishing information obtained through the Internet. The right thing to do is to obtain or confirm the news from qualified, responsible and reliable sources. I verify my articles in prestigious news media, such as CNN, *People*, NBC, *Los Angeles Times*, FOX, CBS, or local media such as *Diario 2001* or the portal *La Patilla,* among others, pages or social networks of the artist, group, character or company organizing shows. If I don't find it there, then I prefer to wait so as not to make the mistake of publishing a *fake news*.

Unfortunately, there are "professionals" or people who think they are journalists simply because they have an account on a social network, and believe they have the right to publish on the Internet[3] , either to increase their visits on their social networks or media for which they work, to gain followers or simply to create some kind of buzz on the networks.

SUCCESS IS SUBJECTIVE

The word success, from my perception, is a stereotypical word used as a synonym for achievement. But what is achievement? Some take it as the opportunity to have achieved a goal, such as publishing a book, buying a Ferrari or working for an overseas news network and settle for that.

I define success as the ability to stick with that goal. If I struggle to achieve a dream, like being a columnist for FOX or CNN, the right thing to do would be to stay with them until I decide to. What's the point of publishing for those news channels if you're going to be fired two months later for not meeting their expectations?

---

3   In journalistic jargon, a pot is a pseudo-news that is not confirmed. It may or may not be true. Most of the time it is fake news.

I once had a person tell me that his greatest success would be to be able to buy a Rolex watch. I didn't understand how something like that could be a success. As I mentioned a million dollar watch or a twenty dollar watch to me is the same thing.

Its function is the same, perhaps the cheaper one will give me more satisfaction, because apart from marking the time, it has other additional functions that the more expensive one does not have, not to mention the peace of mind that I can have to move freely anywhere without fear of being robbed.

I cannot link success with material possessions. Having tranquility, peace and quiet is what really defines success. Material things are superfluous, perishable, sometimes unnecessary. To sleep peacefully every night, without worry, is for me the greatest success. Knowing that I wake up healthy, with the possibility of doing whatever I please, is my greatest achievement.

Have you ever seen children enjoying a bath in the rain in a neighborhood? Have you ever seen that same scene in a rich and famous area? I don't think anyone has ever seen a group of rich kids bathing in the rain while playing in the street.

There are those who have accumulated millions of dollars and bought large mansions with beautiful swimming pools. Sometimes I see those beautiful mansions unoccupied, with those empty pools and the owners submerged in a deep state of depression. Material things do not guarantee happiness and I see it every day.

I can see how the gardener of the millionaire people arrives and performs his work daily. He starts his day early in the morning and at the end of the afternoon he returns home and hugs his wife and children, shares with his friends, they barbecue, have a few beers and at night, he goes to bed and sleeps happily.

Those great millionaires cannot do that, of working their day like any other mortal, coming home and kissing their wives and children and sharing with their friends.

These people distrust everyone because friendships are not sincere, they are formed out of interest. They cannot go out alone for fear of kidnapping, they do not sleep peacefully because they go to bed thinking about their investments, about the rise and fall of their stock price in the stock market, about the pressure of the media, in short, they are people who sacrificed a normal life to become a star belonging to the public and the spectacle.

I do not change the life I lead for the material wealth of those millionaires. I am not saying that having money or property is bad, what is bad is to be consumed by the accumulation of material goods in exchange for tranquility, peace, nights of sleeping pleasantly in my bed for staying up all night working, sacrificing my peace of mind and my mental health.

Success cannot be based on the fulfillment of man's vanities, such as the accumulation of wealth, material possessions or fulfilling a whim to travel into space and take people who want to live on barren worlds, without water, without oxygen, without fertile land, just to see the sun from farther away, when I can enjoy a sunset accompanied by the people I love, on my living planet, still green, despite how polluted it is because of us.

My success is to keep working, which I have achieved in these thirty-seven years at what I once dreamed of as a child, which was writing the news to inform others. My success is to go to bed calmly every night, wake up without worries, write my news, send it out and have the rest of the day to do whatever I want, like walking on the beach, seeing places, enjoying the healthy and positive life, visiting Beto, the crocodile that lives in a pond near my house, watching the sky and the stars lying on the sand. What is your success?

A time will come

in which, with great joy,

you will greet yourself,

to the you who comes to your door,

the one you see in your mirror

and each will smile at the other's welcome,

and say, sit down here. Eat.

You will still love the stranger who was yourself.

Offer wine, offer bread. Return your love

to yourself, to the stranger who loved you

all your life, whom you have never met

to meet another heart

who knows you by heart.

Pick up the cards from the desk,

the photographs, the desperate lines,

peel your image from the mirror.

Sit down. Celebrate your life.

Love after love

Derek Walcott

CHAPTER 7

MY LIFESTYLE

Reader friend, you know me almost as well as I know myself. You know my beginnings, my triumphs, my learning. I hope that my story will serve as an example for you to find your way to success, that success that awaits you and that wants you to be constant with it.

All this path, like a river, has a delta that flows with a purpose: to live happily, that is the life mission of every human being. Although many have lost the path and the reason for their daily struggle, today I remind you that we work to live happily, neither with little, nor with much; with what is necessary.

MY WAY OF LIVING THE LIFE

Now, what remains for me to tell you is how I decided to live life the way I live it. I don't want to say that my style is the best of all, nor do I pretend that you abandon your projects so that you can live a life similar to mine.

The purpose is for you to understand that we can have everything we want without sacrificing what is really essential: our emotional well-being, the days we get to share with the people who are special to us, our material well-being, our physical and mental health, our self-determination, our social inclusion and, above all, respect for our rights.

To begin with, I will tell you that my impetus, my determination, my boldness, have driven me to go after what I want so much: to live in freedom without falling into debauchery.

When I barely turned eighteen I felt like I was emancipated, that I had all the freedom in the world to make my own decisions and indeed, I did.

The first thing was to get my passport so I could travel abroad. The first tourist destination was Aruba, the happy island, as it is also known. The reason for my trip was to celebrate my coming of age.

I remember very well discussing it with a college class-mate. I told him that I had bought a round trip ticket to spend a weekend in Aruba to celebrate my birthday alone.

"Carlos, are you crazy? How can you go to Aruba alone to spend your birthday?" he said, "I'll go with you!"

"But how is it that you're going to accompany me, if I haven't even invited you?"I answered.

"Well, I'll buy a ticket to share with you."

See how daring I was? I didn't mind taking a plane and go-ing abroad alone to celebrate my birthday, far away from everyone, like an explorer facing an unknown world.

Fortunately - because the people who accompany you are fortunate - my friend did travel to Aruba and there I found about twenty other companions. They decided behind my back to go to the happy island to celebrate my eighteenth birthday with me.

Now I ask you, have you ever decided to do something you've always wanted to do, but you're stopped by "a but"? I think it is not worth stopping for any excuse. Always dare to do what you long for, what you dream of, that is the reward that life gives you, that is why we exist: to live.

Of course, maybe because of my parents' influence I am an adventurer. Since I was a child we have always had the habit of traveling. School vacations, Christmas, Carnival, Easter, weekends... there was always a family trip in our itinerary. That tasty habit planted in me that restless spirit that wants to know the world in its entirety.

Today, in my opportunity to live as a resident in the United States, I continue with my lifestyle rooted since childhood: to travel everywhere and see as many places as possible. To achieve my goal I bought a *motor home,* my mobile home to continue with the way of life that my dad taught me.

And the fact is that my way of life is similar to the way Americans live, something that Latin Americans are not used to. That need to explore, to travel, to see new places. There is one thing I like about these people, that every worker thinks about his or her retirement plan.

Who wouldn't like to travel the world once they retire or go into retirement? I think we all would, or at least most of us would.

Wouldn't it be nice to live on a cruise ship and cruise the ocean, knowing that everything is paid for, or live in the tropics? Workers in this country pay into retirement funds to fulfill dreams like the one I just mentioned, especially those who live in states that are very cold in the winter. They seek the summer heat of southern Florida to live out their last years on this material plane.

I, for example, was paying for a monthly retirement package, because one of my dreams is that, when I retire, I want to live on a ship and go to every port in this world, or at least a good part of it.

After a while, I decided not to wait until old age to travel the world, so I bought the *motor home, to get* to know the world from the ground.

However, the idea of sailing in my old age is still alive, so I will soon reactivate my retirement package so that, when I reach the age of a senior citizen, which is not long away, I can make my dream come true and enjoy my last years sailing around the world, with the certainty that I will lack nothing.

WHY DO IT DIFFERENTLY

Many people who know me think that I live in Miami because of my proximity to artists and share their success, fame and pleasures. Nothing so far from reality. I am an entertainment journalist who is oblivious to all the paraphernalia of fashion, fame and fortune.

I have friends in the music industry who have invited me to the *Latin Grammy Awards*. I always say yes, but I never go, until I don't get any more invitations. I prefer to visit a zoo, or some beautiful little town that has a lot of history to tell.

I don't like big cities. If I have to choose between New Orleans and New York, I prefer the former. Big metropolises don't have the appeal I like. I prefer less congested cities, with more historical attractions that tell me their essence. I have already lived in the tumult of buildings and vehicular traffic.

When I visit New Orleans I like to tour its emblematic places, such as the areas where the battles of the American Civil War took place. For example, New England, the deserts of Arizona, Vermont, South Carolina and Pennsylvania among other places.

I like to visit the railroad tracks that linked the north with the south of the country. I also like to visit its museums and get to know part of the colonial legacy of the first inhabitants, the aboriginal redskins or the first settlers.

I have had the opportunity to visit the most representative places, such as Niagara Falls. Beautiful, no doubt, I have been to the beaches of Malibu, in the state of California, and I have seen the mansions of the most famous movie and television stars. In fact, I was living at a friend's house near Matt Damon's house and I saw him jogging on the beach every afternoon, but that doesn't bring me the excitement and joys of visiting a town, the countryside, the beach or the mountains.

The idea is to visit and get to know what fills me the most. I plan my excursions to remote places, few visited with a lot of cultural heritage. I respect those who plan their trips to those big cosmopolitan cities, everyone has the right to go to the place that makes them happiest, that is the idea. And I'm not saying I haven't visited. I love Madrid, Paris, Frankfurt, Barcelona, Bogota, Buenos Aires, among many other cities I have visited. But not to live and have priorities to be there.

Since I got my motor home, when I'm in the mood to travel, I drive late at night, stopping when the moon stops shining on me. That's when I stop. When I wake up, I discover that I am in a spectacular place. I can enjoy a beach sunrise or a sunrise on those great plains in southern Alabama.

In the United States there are places designed to park your RV *(recreational vehicle)*, as *motor homes* are also known. You can leave it in the parking lots of large super-markets such as Walmart, for example, or in exclusive RV zones. I have already toured some of these RV zones in Panama City, in New Orleans, in Alabama and in Georgia, and the road continues. I will be touring the U.S. territory until I get to Tennessee, somewhere around the month of December.

But don't think that now that I live in the United States I do it. I also did it in Venezuela. I traveled much of its extension: from its beautiful beaches in the east, to those picturesque Andean villages in the state of Táchira.

Venezuela has landscapes and places as beautiful or even more beautiful than the U.S. Unfortunately tourism policies have not given the true value to these places and do not promote them. I hope that soon that will change, so I can continue to enjoy the natural wonders of my country and stay there.

Today, as I said before, I am an American resident and soon I will obtain citizenship, but this is not my country. I take advantage of the goodness of its system of govern-ment, of the job opportunities it has given me, but nothing like Venezuela.

Of course, the status I have achieved in this nation has not been a gift. It has been the result of my constant coming and going from Venezuela, thanks to my work as a print media journalist.

I started coming for work since I was nineteen years old. I did it all the time with a photographer named Elio Escalante.

We met models from a modeling agency called *Elite*, owned by John Casablancas. I don't know if it is still active, but they trained beautiful models that later became *top models* like Cindy Crawford, Naomi Campbell, Linda Evangelista, Claudia Schiffer, among others. Of course, we were not lucky enough to interview them, but we did interview others as beautiful as the first ones who walked after success.

Elio worked with them and obtained beautiful photographs for the magazines of the Dearmas Block, such as *Varie-dades* magazine *or Bonita* magazine.

TO BE HAPPY AND SMILE TWENTY-FOUR HOURS A DAY, SEVEN DAYS A WEEK

I am a human being like any other, who suffers and feels what happens in the world. Seeing children crying, hungry and homeless in the streets affects and saddens me, as well as the tragedies that many people live in different parts of the world. As a journalist, I receive all those news that impact human sensibility.

I would like to understand why there are millionaires who prefer to invest their fortunes in the exploration of barren planets for colonization, when they could invest those immense amounts of money in alleviating hunger and thirst in the poorest countries that have served as suppliers of raw materials for the development of their industries.

I have made it a rule to keep all that news from affecting

my mental and emotional health, so I work to live my ife as pleasantly as possible.

You know what I do? I try to infect others with my good mood and good vibes. I tell them that, "in bad weather, good luck", I cheer them up, I try to steal a smile, and when I succeed I tell them that this is what I wanted.

It's been a long, long time since I've felt sad and I thank God for that. There is nothing tastier than going to sleep without worries, without anxiety, without anything to disturb my rest.

If there is something that worries me, I immediately get down to work to solve it. We all have vicissitudes to face and we have to face them and deal with them.

I suffer from them too, I am not immune to them, no human being is. However, as a good administrator of my time, I immediately seek answers to them. Do I achieve something positive by postponing them and dragging my feet? They have to be faced sooner or later and it is best to do it as soon as possible.

Here in the United States, during hurricane season, it rains a lot and the coastal states are regularly hit by these storms. Consequently, every time there is a hurricane in the Caribbean, all the media report on the progress of the storms and make their respective suggestions.

Recently there was a tropical storm threatening the area of Florida where I currently live. Since I know that when they are near, it rains a lot and they suspend electrical service, I took my precautions. Since my *motor home* consists of a motor home and a trailer with a trailer, I anchored the trailer to my car and drove to safety.

That day it rained a lot and the strong winds affected the power lines. The whole area was without electricity. But I was already about forty minutes away from the place, walking through the shopping malls of a city near my home, visiting stores, waiting for the electricity service to be reactivated so I could go back home.

I took precautions, got away from a place that was sure to cause me stress and completely relaxed. I always try to be happy for as long as possible, because if I don't do it myself, who does it for me?

WORK CAN BE A REWARD, NOT A MEANS TO HAPPINESS

Reader friend, at this point in the book you will know that work has given me happiness and the quality of life I have wanted. But has work been my happiness? Definitely not. My professional work in this medium has been a bridge, a path to reach a series of moments that have given me happiness.

Happiness is not to be pursued, it is to be felt because it is always within us. It is not perishable or ephemeral, it is constant and enduring in time.

Happiness is not in achievements nor can it be anchored exclusively in them. I have many personal achievements, but they have not been the most pleasant moments I have had, they have been the small moments that God has given me every day of my life to be happy.

What do I want to tell you with this? That no matter what you do or don't do, you have to make every moment of your life happy. The accumulation of each moment makes a whole called happiness.

I feel that my life has been lived in a circle. I remember the good things that have happened to me, my trip to Argentina, also to the Dominican Republic, Aruba, Curaçao, Peru, Ecuador, Puerto Rico, Bonaire, Brazil, Chile, Colombia, Mexico, Costa Rica, Panama, Europe, to name a few destinations. I remember those pleasant moments in each of my years of life, my visits to those magnificent places that I have been able to know and I realize that each experience adds wonderful things in my life.

There are those who see happiness as an opportunity, like the train that passes by and if you don't board it, you miss it. That is the great mistake of those who think like that. Happiness is forever and the train is always passing by for you to get on it and live it that way.

Stop and see that tiny moment of joy. Are you indulging in a good ice cream? Savor it and enjoy its taste. If you are with someone, enjoy their company, and if you are alone, enjoy your solitude. It's your moment, it's your gift today.

Are you eating a delicious plate of food? Enjoy it and thank God for it. Many people have nothing to eat and you are one of the lucky ones who can. Be thankful for everything you receive each day. From waking up in the morning, to knowing that you are healthy and that your loved ones are well. We are full of little things to be truly happy.

Why do you look for happiness in such big things if it is everywhere? If you choose to do so, depression, stress and anxiety will be your inseparable companions that will embitter your existence.

Whatever you do, put it in God's hands so that it will turn out well. Do not look for happiness in material things, remember the metaphor of the Christmas tree, material things are only ornaments, look for your essence and you will live with joy in your heart.

Live in the moment, enjoy what you have, learn to laugh and you will see how everything around you will fill you with joy. There are a couple of anecdotes that corroborate what I am telling you. When I was a child, because I was having my little run around and running around, I fell and got a very deep wound that required six stitches. I remember that, at the hospital, my mother used to tell me: "laugh, mijo, because what happened to you was for something, so laugh and don't cry".

Since then I have not stopped seeing the good in the bad things. So much so that after my escapades in the Dearmas Block, I was often greeted the next day with a strong wake-up call.

They would give me those lectures and I would smile from ear to ear. They would call me "hard face" for that reaction while scolding me. It's not that I'm crazy, it's just that my mom programmed me to laugh at all times, even if it's unpleasant.

I am so clueless in that regard that sometimes I am not careful about what I say. When I go to funerals, I prepare myself psychologically so I don't screw up with my comments. I may say to the family member of the deceased, "congratulations on your loss."

I once had a traffic accident in Venezuela on my way to work. I fell asleep while driving, the car lost control and overturned on the road. I don't know how I got out of that accident unscathed.

The crash was so severe that the car's insurance declared it a total loss. Imagine, it was a Caribbean van and it was completely wrecked.

Upon arrival of the competent authorities, they were surprised to see me conscious and without a scratch. I explained that I had fallen asleep and that I had not affected anyone else. I called the insurance company and the towing service and when they arrived, I left everything in the hands of the insurance broker and went to work, as if nothing had happened.

What could I do, mourn? No, I went on with my routine and said "God will provide". At that time I was working at the Eurobuilding Hotel, in Caracas, with the Rembrandt de Venezuela cosmetics people. The owner, Dr. Alessandro Nocerino, heard about my crash and that I had lost my vehicle.

Since he was a horse racing enthusiast and owned his own horses, he told me that if his horse won at the races, he would give me a car.

At that time, I had a friend who was selling a 1974 Ford Fairlane 500, and I wanted that one. Imagine, I was so crazy that I didn't want a new car, but an old one; I wanted it because it reminded me of Batman's car. It was a long and sturdy car, it looked more like a boat with wheels than a car.

The day of the race I went into a betting shop to watch the race that was going to be broadcasted and when the horse left, I was pushing the fast horse with my mind. "Run like the wind, Latino Venezolano!". That was the name of that bolide that ate up the track like lightning, thus winning the race.

As promised, Dr. Nocerino bought the vehicle from my friend for cash and gave it to me with great affection, something for which I will be grateful for the rest of my life.

As you will see, joy is not in material things but in what makes us really happy, and that car was one more reason for my happiness. The older the car, the greater my joy. Surely if they gave me a donkey cart I would be the happiest man on the planet.

To close this chapter, I will leave you as a gift a beautiful poem by Pablo Neruda that encapsulates what I have shared with you throughout this book.

Live in the moment and be happy with what you have!

This time let me

be happy,

nothing has happened to anyone,

I am nowhere to be found,

happens only

that I am happy

on all sides

of the heart, walking,

sleeping or writing.

What can I do, I'm happy.

I am more innumerable

that the grass

in the meadows,

my skin feels like a rough tree

and the water below,

the birds above,

the sea as a ring

on my waist,

made of bread and stone the earth

the air sings like a guitar...

...Today let me

to me alone

be happy,

with all or without all,

be happy

with the grass

and sand,

be happy

with the air and the earth,

be happy,

with you, with your mouth,

be happy.

Ode to a Happy Day

Pablo Neruda

I am a poet: I feel in my brain

the inspiration boils, the idea vibrates;

I feel it radiating in my exalted mind

images as bright as stars.

The scorching fire of volcanoes

in my giant heart flames;

I climb the sky, I descend into the abysses,

I roar in the sea, I ride in the storm.

I am a poet: my spirit escapes

from the petty prison of the earth,

and about other spaces and other worlds

spreads its wings like a haughty eagle.

Drink the light in the lightning mansion;

"traverses the ethereal orbits",

and the penetrating harpoon of their pupils

the panorama of the sphere.

I am a poet: to the murmur of nations

the strings of my zither are tempered;

I weep in the black world of the tombs,

river in the bacchanal, thunder in the war.

Love and homeland are my life;

the human heart, my poem;

my religion, charity and art;

sublime freedom my flag.

I am a poet: I feel in my brain

the inspiration boils, the idea vibrates;

I feel it radiating in my exalted mind

brilliant images: I am a poet!

Poem *Introduction*

Manuel Reinas

CHAPTER 8

WHEN THE HEART DOES THE WRITING

ere I will leave you a nice anecdote about my beginnings in poetry and my dream to publish a book with my poems. It is no secret to tell you that, since my childhood, I have been in love with writing; at that time I used to transcribe the songs of my favorite artists. Years went by and a romantic fervor for the written word grew in my chest and without realizing it, I started to produce some verses and some rhymes. Little by little I immersed myself in poetry and by my twenties I had written more than three hundred poems.

Whenever I could, I wrote. I was inspired by life, my love for God, the stories of love and heartbreak born from my fantasies, the stories of love and heartbreak of others, such as those of my relatives, friends or acquaintances.

I listened to their pitiful stories, their victories and failures, their motivations, their actions of faith and hopes, and I kept feeding myself with topics to continue writing. I filled notebook after notebook and kept them, accumulating them. It was the radiographic record of the time that was marked in my memories and that I did not want to lose.

Thus I went on writing and thus I accumulated poem after poem; notebook after notebook, until one day, without realizing it, time and action left me working as a news editor, immersed between the pages of magazines, newspapers, in an environment of editors.

I was seduced by the editorial passion of my work environment, which gave rise to the idea of publishing my poems. As I wanted to know if they were publishable, I took some of those poems stored in those old notebooks and I cleaned them up.

Rosana Ordóñez, who today is in the clouds and enjoying the goodness of the Kingdom of God, who was the person who gave me the opportunity to work in the Dearmas Block, was the one who told me that it was a material worthy of publication. Journalists such as Aquilino José Mata and Apolinar Martínez, who at the time was the director of the *Meridiano* newspaper, also read my poems, and they also supported me and fanned the flame that was burning in my chest.

After so much praise and support from my co-workers and my bosses, I began to look for information about publishers that could publish this type of genre, among them came the names of Editorial Planeta, and the people from the Dearmas block, through Distribuidora Continental, the people in charge of publishing their books.

By that time I was working with *Mariela's New Style* models and model Ronny Raniolo, who had participated in a fashion show of designer Gianni Versace in Milan, Italy. Ronny was a supermodel at the time and lived in Valencia. The photographs of the models with him gave my magazines a *plus* on the covers.

To take advantage of the image that this boy had as a recognized model, I would escape with my photographer friends to the agency of Mariela Centeno and Tiby Rivas, in the company of Ronny. We would work in long photo sessions, after finishing my activities at the headquarters of the editorial complex. They always took good pictures in each publication, which made them grow as models in the fashion world. It was a very profitable symbiosis that we had.

On one occasion, we were working on a photo shoot in El Hatillo, a town east of Caracas. When I finished with the photographs, I asked Ronny to take me to Coche, a sector in the south of the city that was a strategic point for hitchhiking to the city of Los Teques, where I lived. Since he lived in Valencia, he didn't mind dropping me off in that area because it was on his way.

I used to carry my poems up and down. I was still looking for a publisher to publish them. Although I had already made some progress with Distribuidora Continental, I always carried them with me in case another opportunity arose.

When Ronny gave me a ride to Coche, I put the booklet under the carpet of the passenger seat so I wouldn't have to carry it in my hands, it was like an impulse to keep it safe. It was my most precious treasure, I already saw myself as an official poet, it was a dream that was about to come true.

Ronny had his vehicle for sale, but a buyer interested in buying his nice car had yet to show up. I, being absent-minded, forgot the poems under the seat and it wasn't until I got home that I realized I had left them. It was Friday, between my exhaustion from work and the relaxation of the weekend I forgot to call him at home to tell him to keep the poems for me.

The next day I told Ronny that I had forgotten the poetry book under the passenger seat, that if he lifted the carpet he would find them. He always kept his car spotless and to my misfortune, that weekend he was able to sell the car. He received a call from a person who was interested in buying the car from him, they arranged to meet, check it out and finalize the sale.

When I called him he told me that he had sold the car and in the buyer's inspection he saw nothing extra, except for the spare rubber and the toolbox. That was how I lost more than three hundred poems and it was also how I was discouraged to publish the rest of the poems that were in other notebooks, all piled up, under a batch of foreign magazines that I bought and collected.

Although I had already overcome the issue of publishing my poems, years after that mishap I tried to write more, but they no longer flowed as before. I had a hard time starting them, and if I did, I had a hard time finishing them. I felt that the muse was not with me and that I did not have the same fervor of previous years.

But things have a perfect time to consolidate. In the elaboration of this book I felt again that illusion of publishing them, but I had not written any other after that incident.

As God would have it, I had a revealing dream that told me that there was a notebook with several of my poems written by that time, besides the ones I had lost in Ronny's car. In my dream I saw how I found a notebook under some magazines that were stored in an old wooden trunk that I have in my house, back in Los Teques.

When I woke up, I called my brother in Venezuela and asked him to look in the old trunk for that notebook I had seen in my dreams, which I was sure was under a group of German magazines I collected. Indeed, my brother found the notebook and took pictures of each of its pages.

This is how this last chapter came about, because after finding my poems, it occurred to me that this book could announce my next publication: a book of poetry. A dream come true that will reveal the feelings that can only be dictated by the heart and show that one should not stop dreaming and that one should not get impatient if one works on the consolidation of dreams.

Now I share with you, my friend reader, some of my first poems and it will be like an appetizer for the next ones to read. I thank you for having accompanied me on this journey. From now on you will only read part of this dream come true: the written voice of my soul, of my heart overflowing with joy, for the culmination of a dream and the beginning of another, "one that carries the soul of the world", as Benedetti said when defining poetry, "one that allows to remember something forgotten", according to Francis H. Bradley and "to reach the aesthetic experience", well defined by Borges.

To you, my reader friend, simply,

Thank you!

I don't know if I am mortal or immortal

What I do know is that there are those

that have reversed roles.

There are those who live by the death of others

and there are others who die for the life of those.

I am more afraid of moral suffering than physical suffering.

I feel like the void,

because emptiness is nothing;

since it is nothing, it could not exist,

for if there were a vacuum

I would go there

to mourn my suffering,

but, of course, I have somewhere to go.

The boundary between you and me has a way of being crossed.

the wisest thing is to be able to cross over,

come without prejudices and customs,

see no dividing lines.

I wait for you with the illusion of a lifetime.

I wait for you with a fed desire;

You just need to decide to cross the border between you and me.

When you touch me my skin lights up.

I don't know what's wrong with you,

your fingers look like fire,

your kisses too.

Your caresses burn me,

are firewood burning in me.

Then...

I want more and more,

red-hot.

North I go.

I go up to heaven.

Your love burns my bonfire.

Your gestures illuminate me like the sun.

I don't know what's wrong with me,

but when you're next to me

my body burns.

The beauty of virtue

I don't know what name I would give it,

you are not a virgin.

Your face is not common and your voice is not human.

Your body shines like a sugar candy,

and your sunny eyes sparkle like gold.

What difference does it make?

Me so immortal and you so distant from others....

My life without you has no reason

I only have one illusion,

a hope,

a hint of love,

just a gesture from you,

but I receive tasteless words

that I season with action

and it is that this is

a love that I alone know,

something infinitely mine.

You are pure genius.

When you look up, the sun gains strength.

When you look down, the earth lies at your feet.

When you look at me my heart bursts with passion

and drop by drop my blood totals my hopes,

my idyll and my will to live.

Every drop is invigorating,

stimulates my intellect, stirs my desires,

pours down the stream a thousand sensations of passion;

and it's not a whim, it's the force of love...

Your silence hurts

and you don't know.

Your words are hollow and empty,

but they echo in me.

Your caresses are reduced to compliments,

do not go any further.

Uncertainty?

Coincidence?

What I am sure of

is that for your love I live and die at the same time.

Today, as always, you are my accomplice.

Wonderful magic moon.

You know my fears, my disappointments,

you know the meaning of each of my tears.

Tell me, O moon, what shall I do with this life?

You who know everything, tell me, what do you think of me?

Answer my questions because I am silent!

I know how to keep this secret quiet...

Today, magical dream ball,

guide my steps

I don't know where I'm going anymore

and I'm afraid to die chasing dreams

slowly, very slowly...

There is a storm in my whole body,

it is time to live, to live intensely.

I had been asking God for a long time

would grant me a gesture of love from you

and a gesture broke that complaint,

ended the anguish, the insecurity.

Subtly your lips touched mine,

since then my dark sky has stars.

I love the love we give each other,

so kiss me long and hard,

now and in the hour of our lives.

Amen!

Your image is vital.

Your smile and the way you look

are the elements that nourish my existence.

You are to me as water is to fish,

my wings to fly.

It is my life and my love for you greater than existence itself.

Without you life loses all meaning

for all my senses lead to you.

There are feelings without names,

without vocabulary,

without meaning,

without words.

When I think of you

sadness embraces my whole being,

makes me understand,

friendship goes up in smoke.

Unreal and calculating you turned out to be

like the rest of the mortals

you played with the pain from the corner.

As a child I tremble in the dense darkness

and even in full light I shudder.

It's not that I'm afraid of full light,

is that my love has turned into darkness,

in darkness.

*I do not know how to distinguish between what is harmful
and what is desirable.*

I don't walk in the right direction,

*I don't sleep well, and I don't do my chores as they
should be.*

Not even this that I write

*stops the penetration of your thought into my human
thought.*

I only think of my treasure,

the most valuable, without underestimating other riches.

It is that my love for you has no limits;

but if you want you can brighten the daylight.

Since I've been with you

the tears dried up,

I am another, I am happy,

fears are gone,

loneliness took another course.

Since I've been with you

my life is different.

Now I understand what dreaming is,

I recognize the importance of time,

I am another, I am happy.